Renée C. Byer

A Mother's Journey and Selected Photographs

North Gallery
Samuel Dorsky Museum of Art
2010

This book is being published on the occasion of the exhibition *Renée C. Byer: "A Mother's Journey" and Selected Photographs*, curated by Brian Wallace and on display in the North Gallery of the Samuel Dorsky Museum of Art from January 30 – April 11, 2010.

This exhibition of new and recent works by Ms. Byer was organized in collaboration with the Department of Communication and Media's annual James H. Ottaway Sr. Endowed Visiting Professorship in Journalism program, for which Ms. Byer served as the 2010 Visiting Professor.

Major support for the exhibition was provided by:
James H. Ottaway Sr. Endowed Professorship of Journalism
Department of Communication and Media
College of Liberal Arts and Sciences
Friends of the Samuel Dorsky Museum of Art

Support for this publication was provided by:
Arthur Anderson
James H. Ottaway, Jr. and Mary Ottaway

This publication is a joint undertaking of the Samuel Dorsky Museum of Art and the Journalism Program of the Department of Communication and Media, State University of New York at New Paltz.

Published by the Samuel Dorsky Museum of Art
State University of New York at New Paltz
One Hawk Drive
New Paltz, New York 12561

Coordinated by Arthur Zaczkiewicz ('96)

Printed and distributed by www.lightningsource.com
ISBN No. 978-0-615-35845-1

Introduction

Brian Wallace, Curator

Ms. Byer, who grew up in the mid-Hudson Valley and was the winner of the 2007 Pulitzer Prize in photojournalism, is the ninth James H. Ottaway Sr. Endowed Professorship of Journalism at the State University of New York at New Paltz.

Ms. Byer won her Pulitzer Prize, the top award in journalism, for "A Mother's Journey," an intimate portrayal of a single mother's emotional and financial struggle as her son battled neuroblastoma, a rare form of childhood cancer. "When done well," said Ms. Byer, "photojournalism is a powerful tool because it connects people to the reality of life and can bring understanding and awareness to important issues." This exhibition includes thirty works from "A Mother's Journey."

The exhibition also includes a selection of other works—single photographs and images from other series—completed by the artist in recent years. The projects included in this grouping address, among other issues, the political, ethical, and personal aspects of hunger, disease, and the uneven distribution of wealth.

Photojournalism and so-called fine art photography, so often defined in contrast to one another, co-exist uneasily in the spaces of the museum. The contemplation invited by art can seem quite different form the urgency created by journalism; the terms with which images and subjects from one area are discussed can seem useless when applied to the other; career paths for art or journalism photographers can seem radically divergent. This exhibition represents an opportunity for a range of people—on the campus and in the community—to explore together the powers and limits of photography and the image.

Renée C. Byer is currently Senior Photojournalist at the Sacramento Bee (California), one of the nation's top newspapers. She won her Pulitzer Prize, the top award in journalism, for a year-long series of photographs of a single mother and her 10 year-old son who was dying of cancer.

Ms. Byer explains the genesis of "A Mother's Journey" as well as how much time she spent with Cyndie French and Derek Madsen:

"The project began after I met Cyndie French at a 'Race for the Cure' event and discovered that her youngest son had been diagnosed with neuroblastoma five months before," Ms. Byer says. "She invited me to visit them and tell their story. Several weeks later I visited them at home and that began my one year journey documenting their lives. I was impressed with a single mom who had very little, but gave so much love and devotion to her son. My focus was that billions of dollars go to cancer research, but very little to help families through the emotional and financial challenges to allow them the time to spend with their dying child. Through the eyes of Cyndie French and Derek Madsen, 10, we can see that this could have been the most precious gift in the most vital moment."

"I'm so grateful the family invited me into their lives to do this story," Ms. Byer says. "Not that many families would allow that. I felt that it was my compassion, patience, honesty and sensitivity that gained me the access to do this story. I feel when people let you into their lives it's a gift and that you have to honor and respect their space. Sometimes that meant not making photos."

Racing barefooted after kicking off her flip-flops, Cyndie French, 39, pushes her son Derek Madsen,10, up and down hallways in the UC Davis Medical Center in Sacramento on June 21, 2005, successfully distracting him during the dreaded wait before his bone marrow extraction. Cyndie had to beg and cajole him to get Derek here. Doctors want to determine whether he is eligible for a blood stem cell transplant, his best hope for beating neuroblastoma, a rare childhood cancer, which was diagnosed in November 2004.

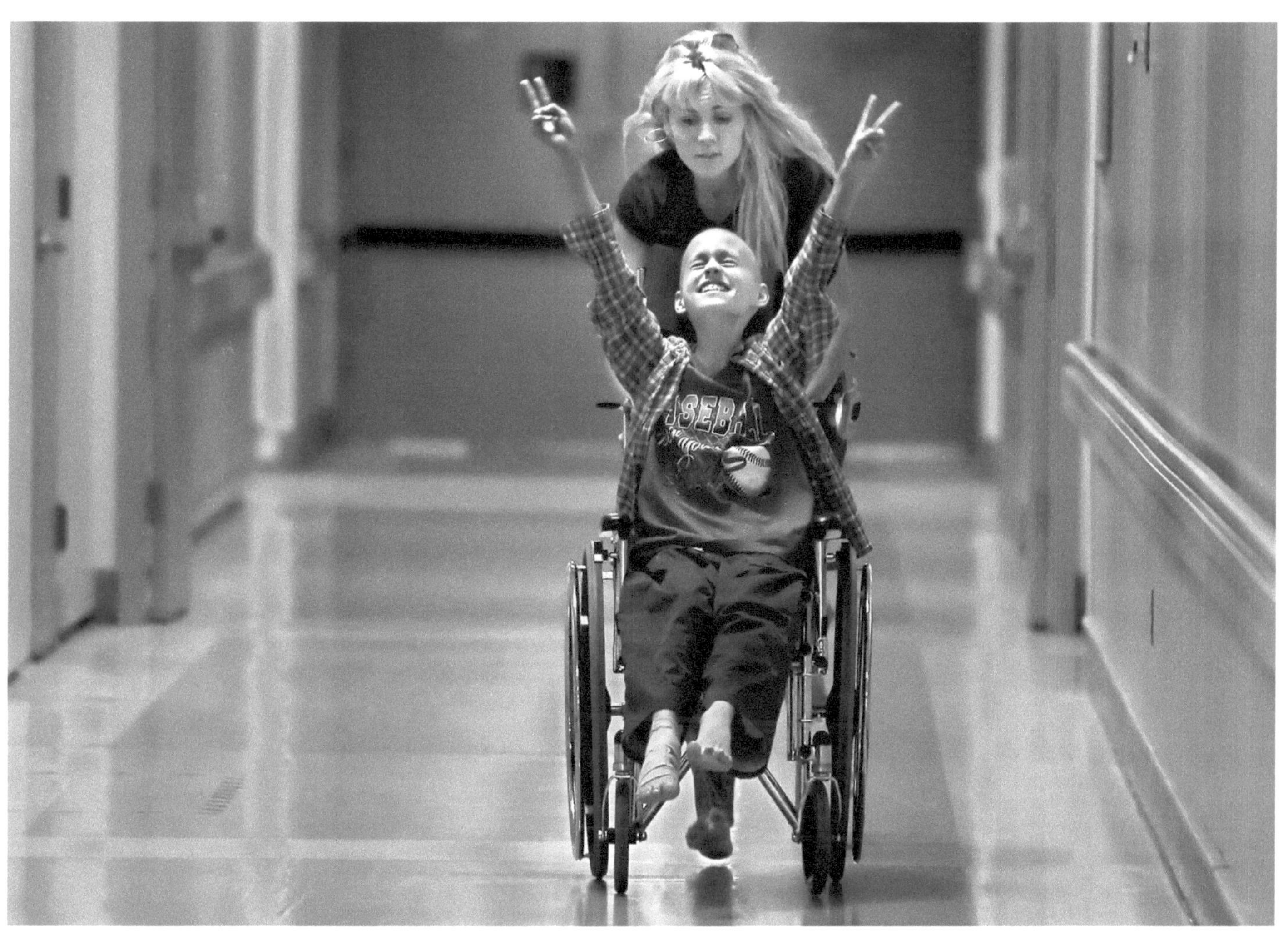

Cyndie French, embraces her son, Derek Madsen, 10, on July 25, 2005, after learning Derek needs surgery to remove a cancerous tumor in his abdomen. The emotional impact is taking its toll on her. "How can anyone maintain a nine-to-five job and do this?" she begins to wonder.

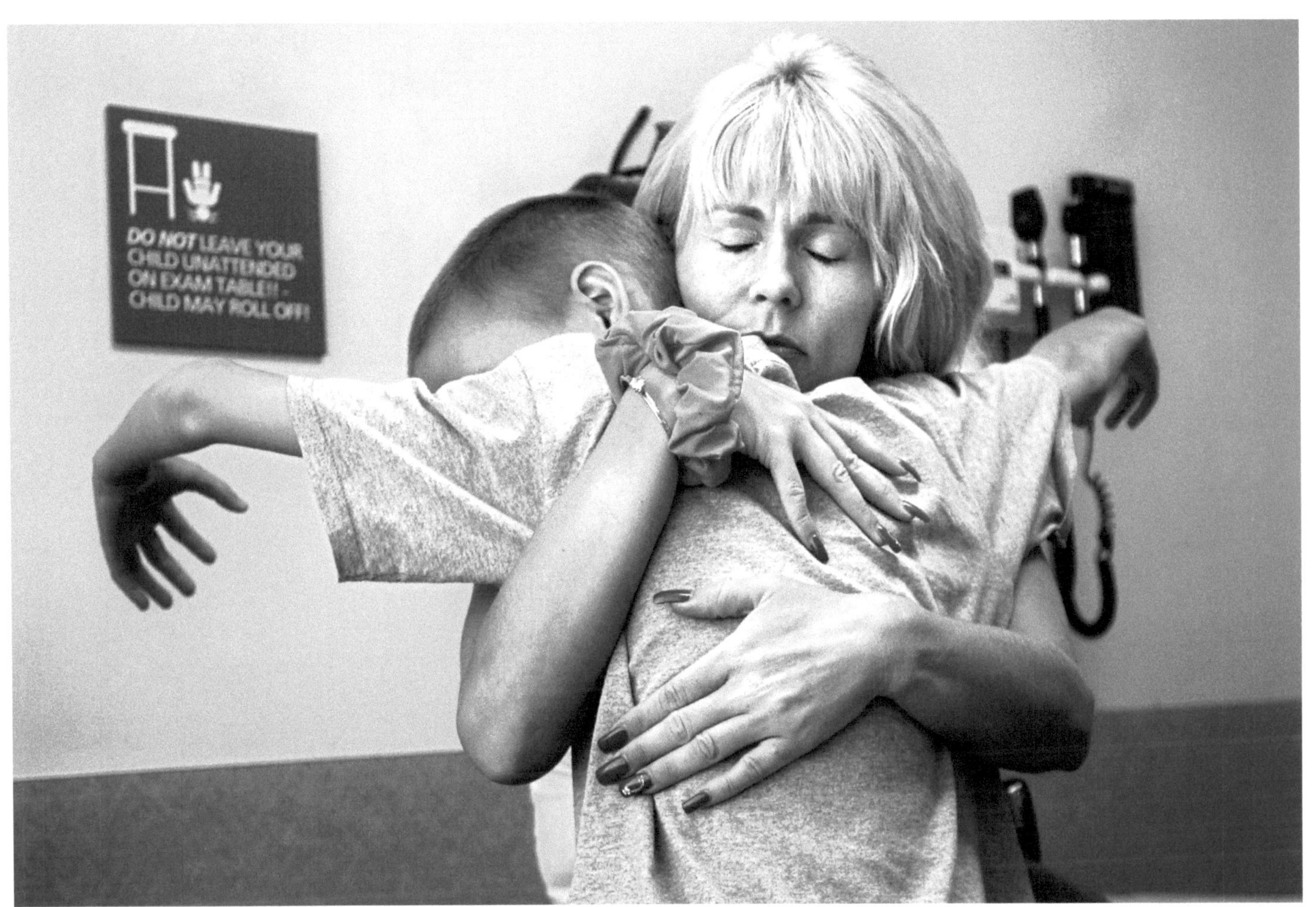
DO NOT LEAVE YOUR
CHILD UNATTENDED
ON EXAM TABLE!! -
CHILD MAY ROLL OFF!

Derek Madsen, 10, gets a soothing massage from his mother, Cyndie French, at her Sacramento nail and tanning salon. "I'm going to do whatever it takes to make him happy, to see him smile." Cyndie says. A single mom of five, Cyndie had to give up her salon at a financial loss to care for her dying son.

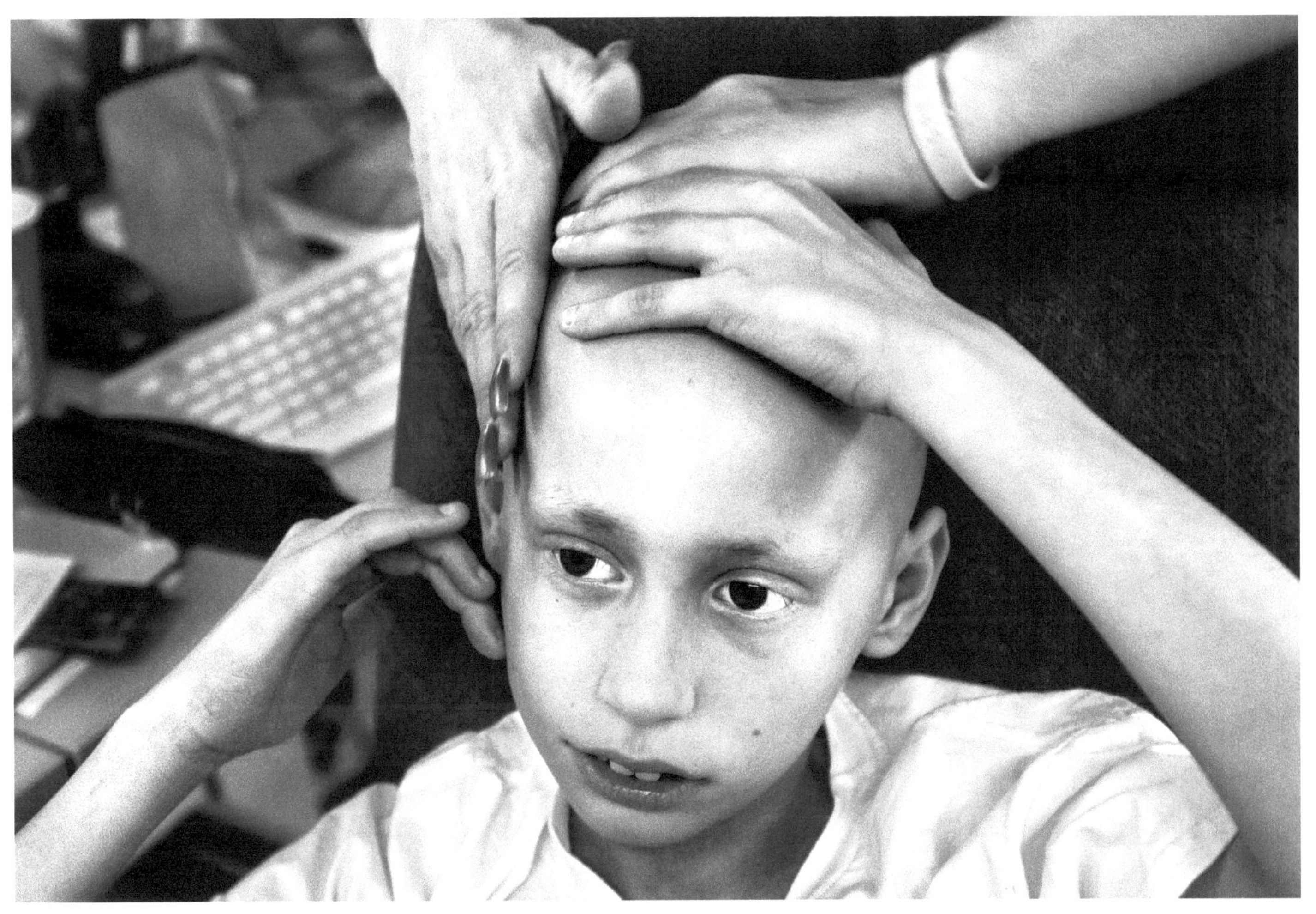

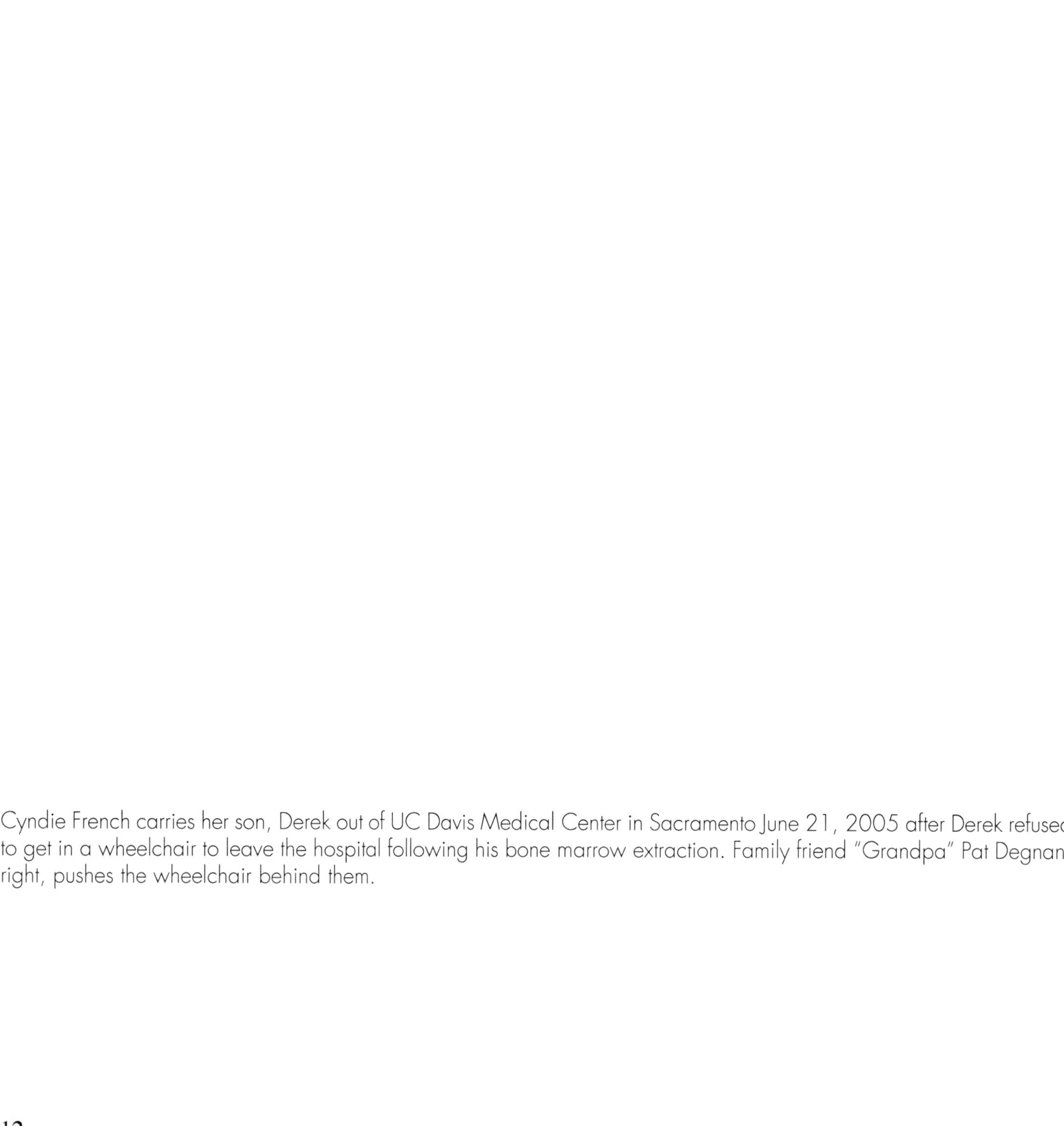

Cyndie French carries her son, Derek out of UC Davis Medical Center in Sacramento June 21, 2005 after Derek refused to get in a wheelchair to leave the hospital following his bone marrow extraction. Family friend "Grandpa" Pat Degnan, right, pushes the wheelchair behind them.

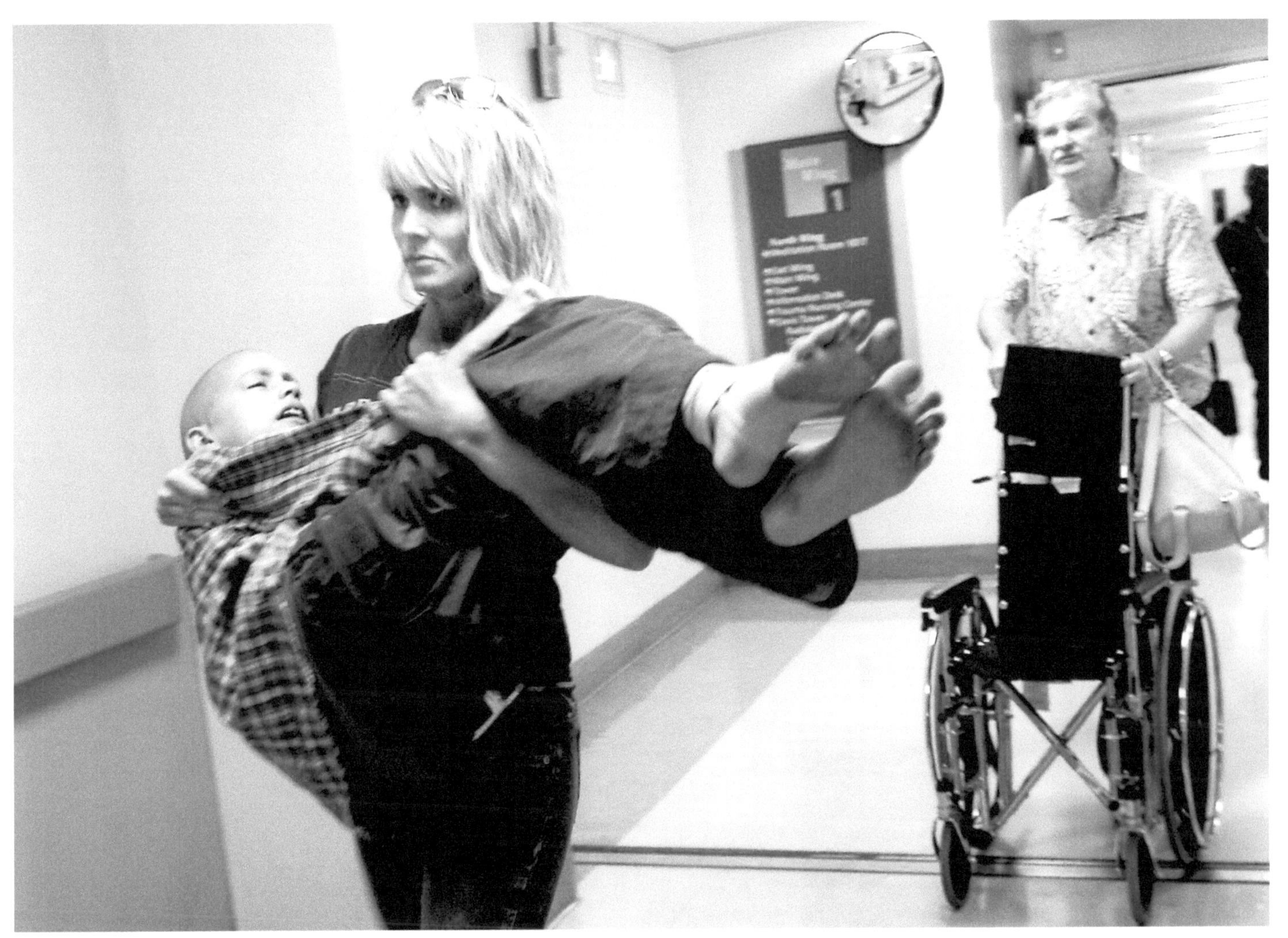

Derek Madsen, center, jumps between beds at a Lake Tahoe hotel on July 16, 2005 with his brother Micah Moffe, left, and best friend RJ Dolan. The trip provided by NBA star Chris Webber marks Derek's first time staying in a hotel. Micah later jokes that his younger brother's favorite saying during the weekend was, "Put it on my tab." Their mom Cyndie French, who accompanied the boys to Tahoe, had contacted Webber and other celebrities in her efforts to make every moment memorable for Derek.

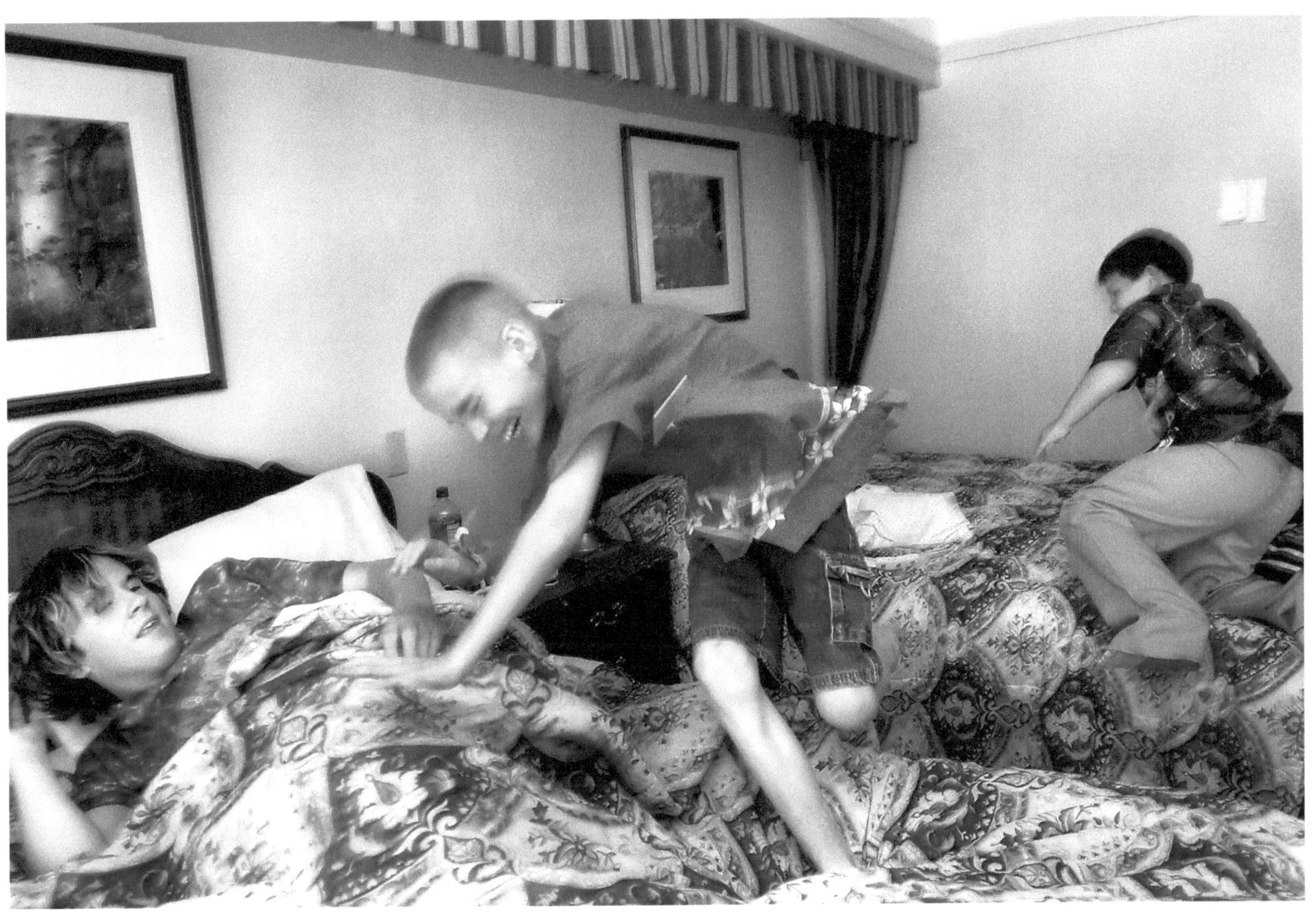

After learning that a hospital check-in has been moved back four hours on July 27, 2005, Cyndie frantically tries to work out a way to get Derek to UC Davis Medical Center while avoiding one of his meltdowns.

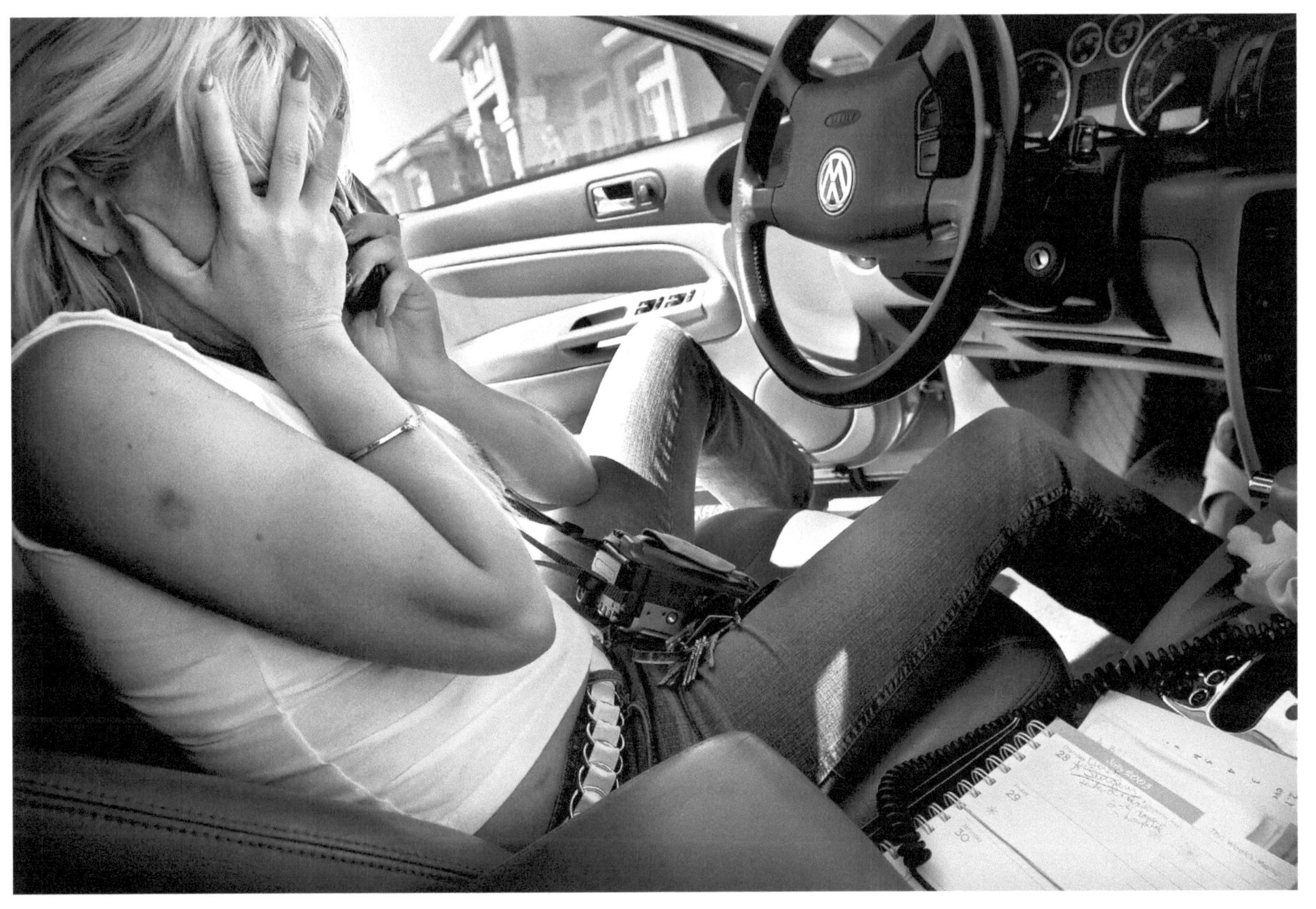

Derek playfully taunts his mother as Cyndie tries to coax him down from a wall outside the UC Davis Medical Center in Sacramento. They are there to admit Derek for cancer surgery the following day. Cyndie, who understands Derek's emotional meltdown before procedures, spends hours getting him in the door of the hospital.

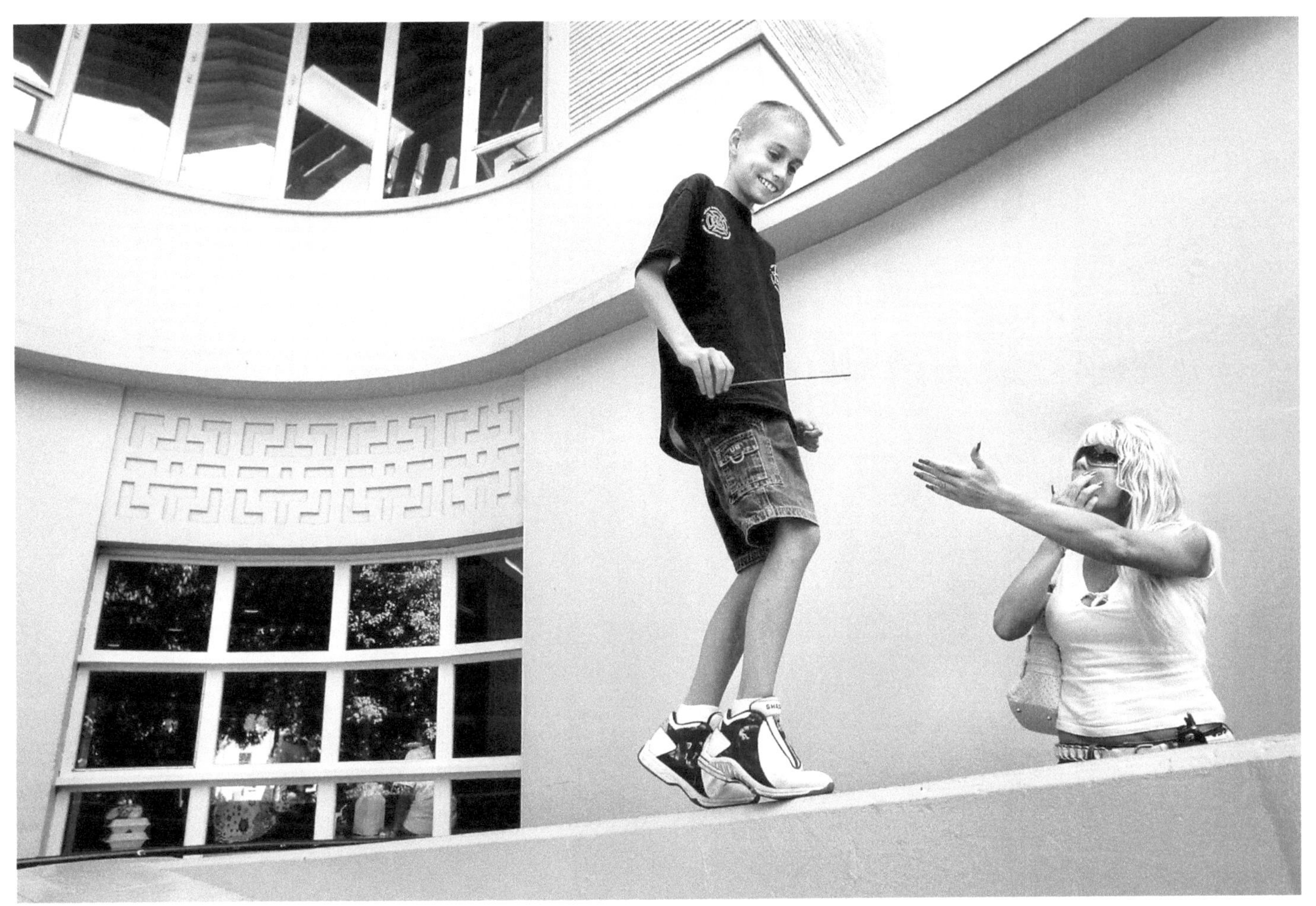

Cyndie French, center, intensely watches as nurses prepare her son Derek Madsen, 10, for a tumor removal surgery at UC Davis Medical Center on July 28, 2005. Although Cyndie talked her way into the preparation for the surgery she was not allowed to view the surgery.

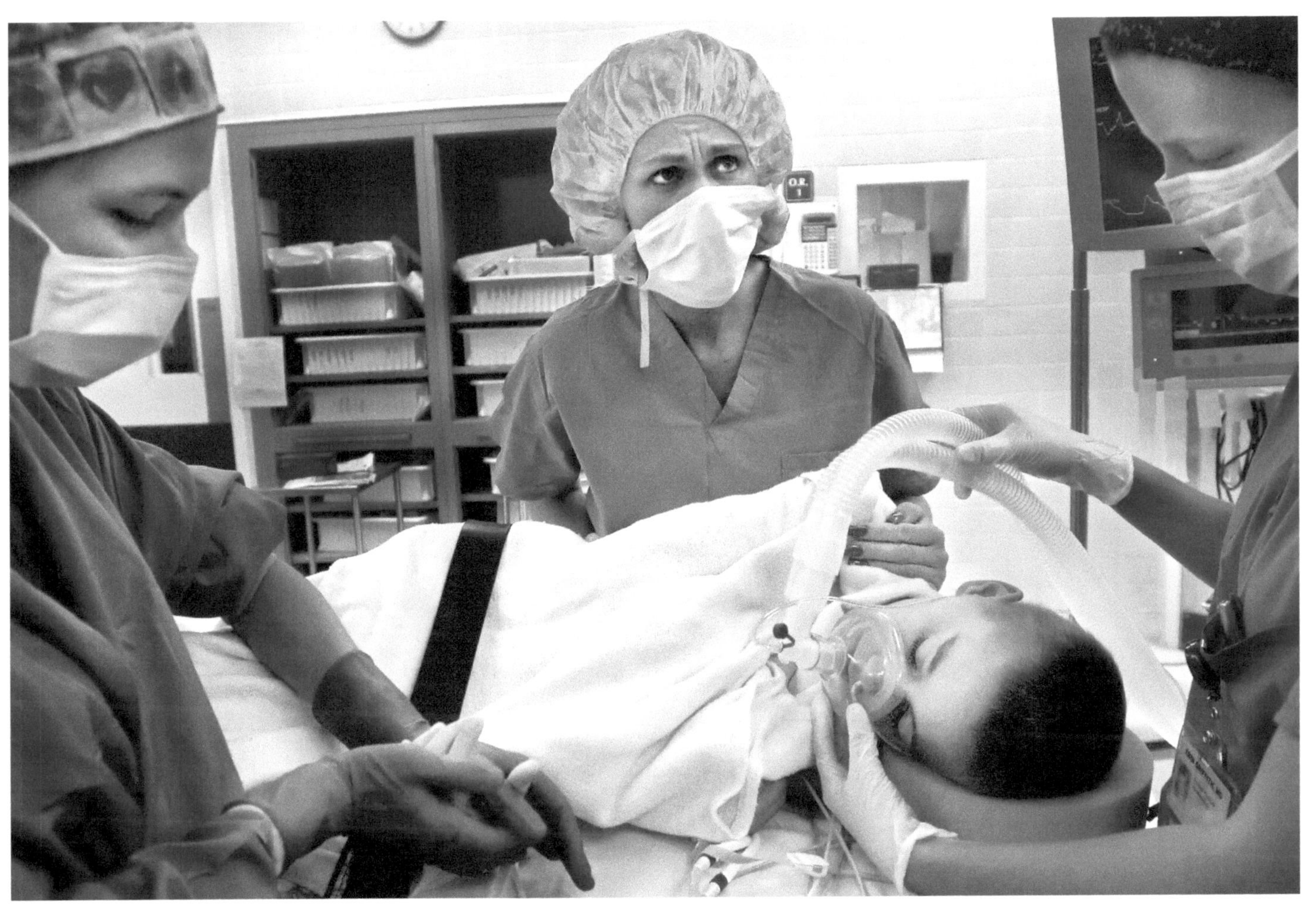
O.R.
1

Shortly after his 11th birthday and Cyndie's 40th, Derek is comforted by his brother Micah Moffe, 17, left, and mom Cyndie, right, as he gets a tattoo in preparation for radiation therapy on November 30, 2005. Micah often accompanies Derek to treatments even though his schoolwork suffers.

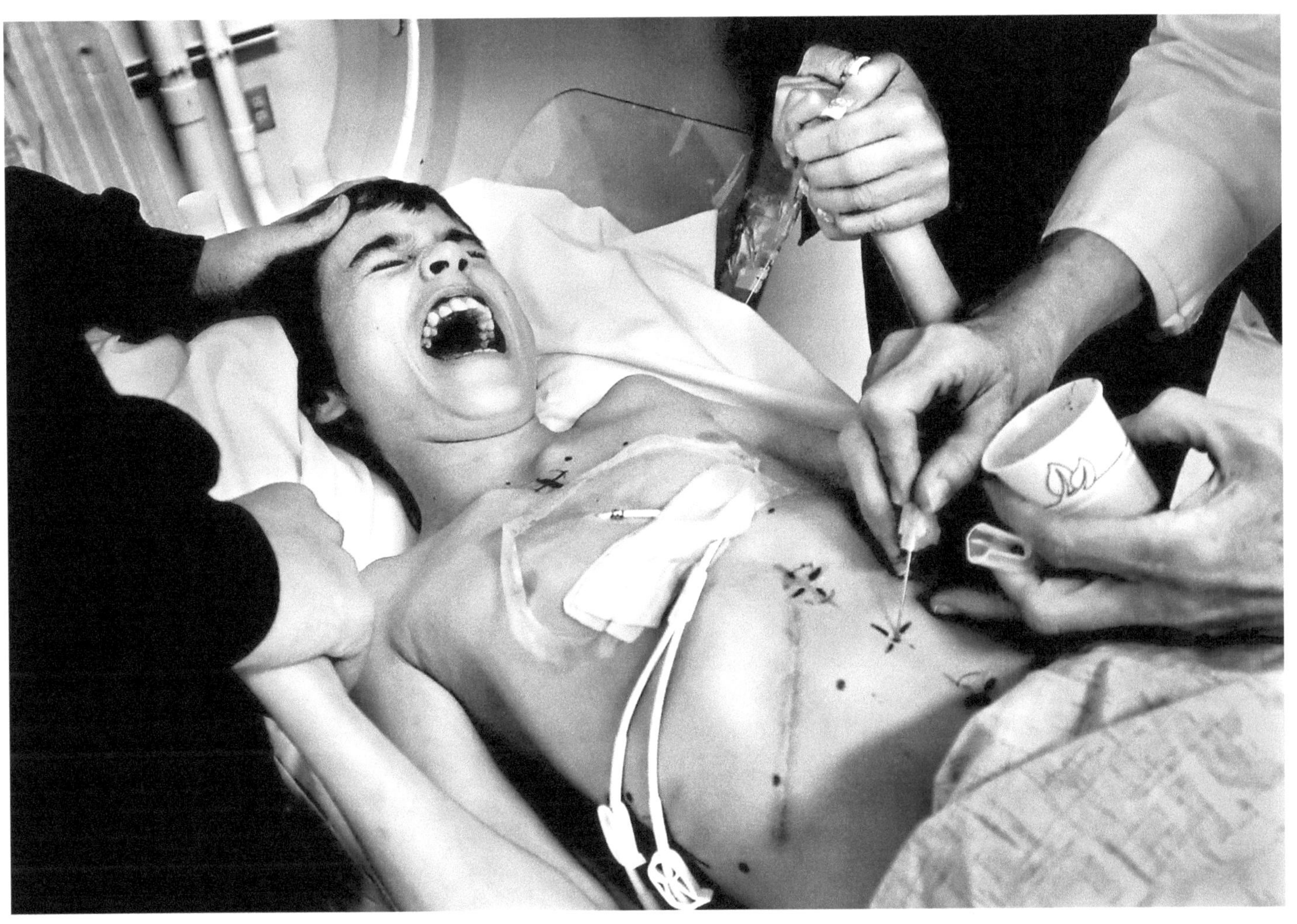

Cyndie French parades a photo collage of her son Derek before students at River City High School in West Sacramento on April 13, 2006, as she seeks volunteers to help with the American Cancer Society's Relay for Life. She also asks for help with a barbecue benefit in her son's honor to help with family expenses.

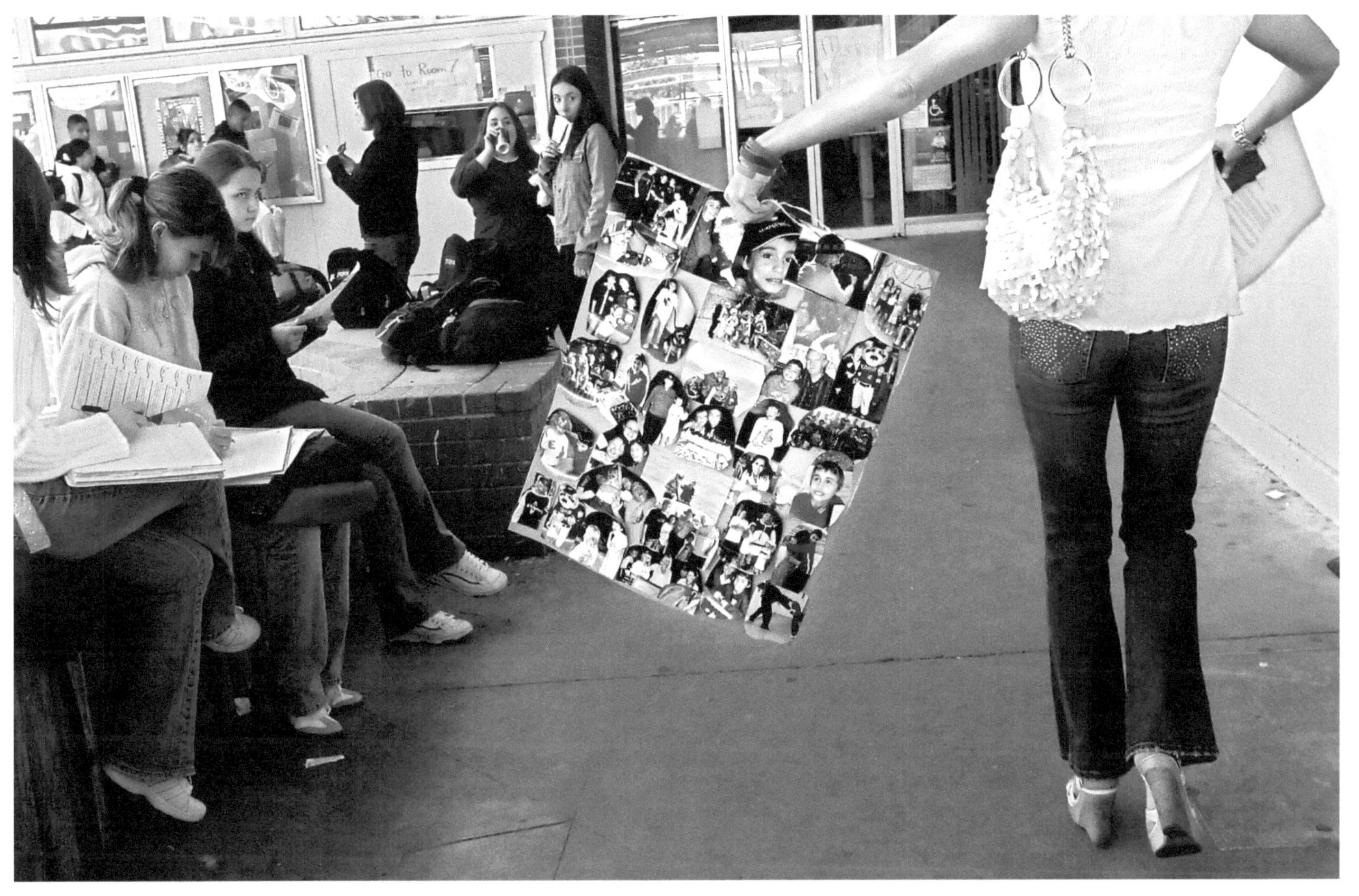
Go to Room 7

On February 6, 2006, one of Derek's cancer doctors recommends Cyndie contact hospice workers. She doesn't tell Derek about the conversation, but retreats behind a closed door at home to cry. "I don't think it's important to tell him," she says. "Why? What for?" Sensing her sadness, Derek tries to cheer up his mom.

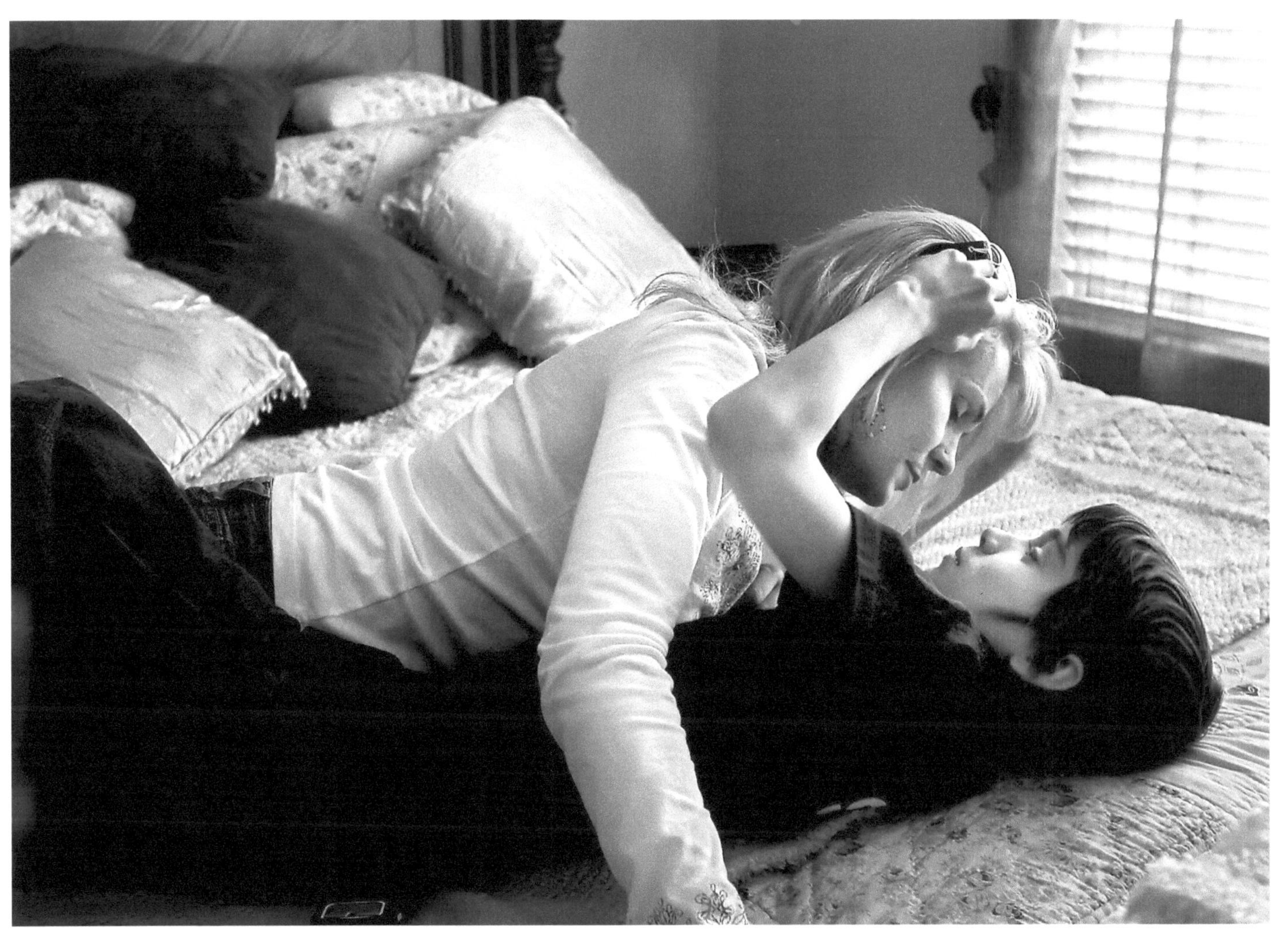

Realizing that Derek may never have an opportunity to get his driver's license, something he's told her he is anticipating, Cyndie French defies the rules and lets him drive up and down their street in West Sacramento. On the same day, Feb. 9, 2006, Cyndie met for the first time with hospice workers, and learns there is little time left for Derek.

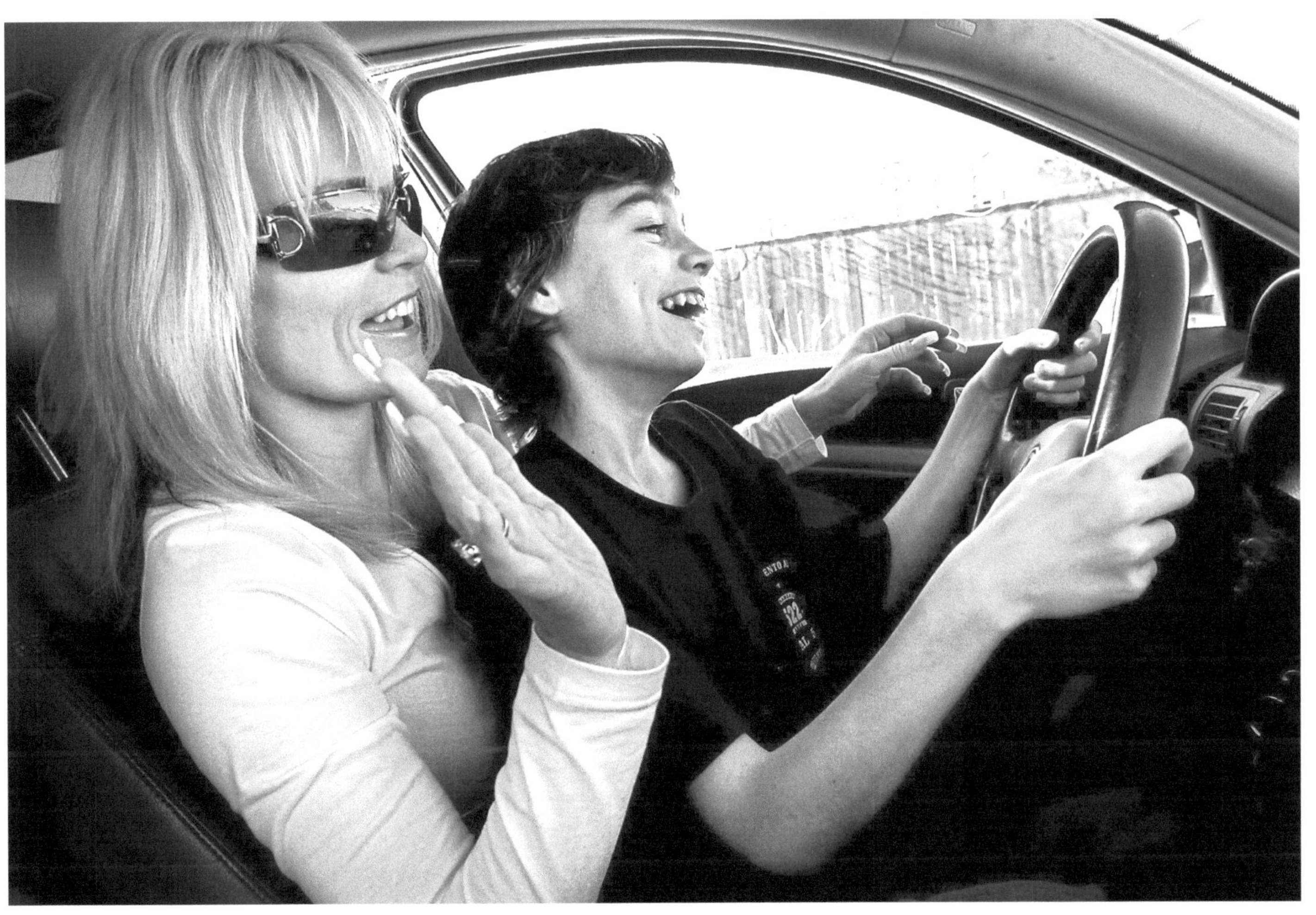

Derek is tearful as Cyndie tries to reason with him at the UC Davis Cancer Center on Feb. 14, 2006. She and Dr. William Hall argue that Derek should have a series of radiation treatments to shrink tumors spreading throughout his body and alleviate his pain. "Derek, you might not make it if you don't do this," Cyndie tells her son. Derek fires back: "I don't care! Take me home. I'm done, Mom. Are you listening to me? I'm done."

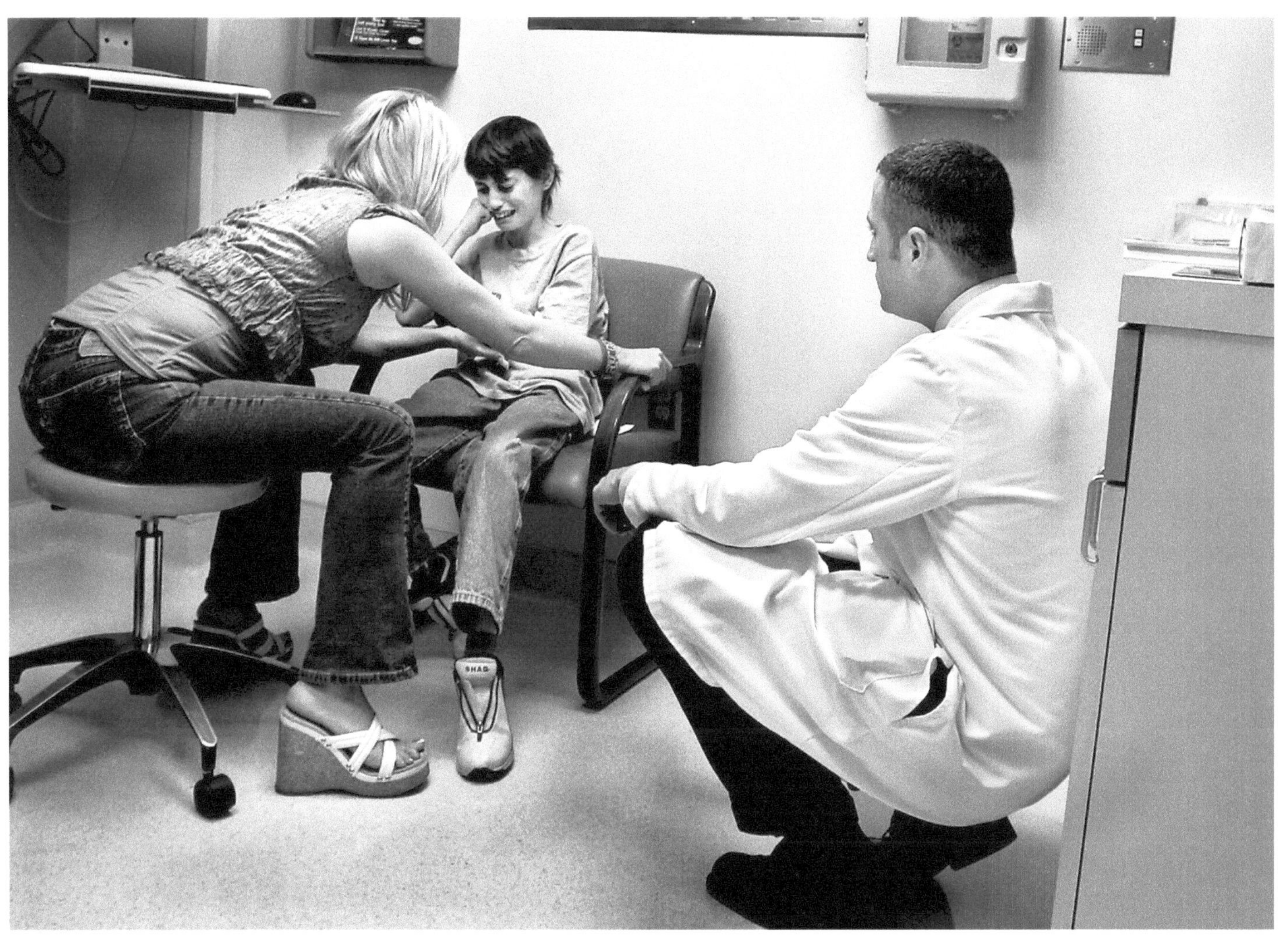

Cyndie French and her son, Derek count the $481 and change collected at the car wash by relatives and friends to assist the West Sacramento family late in the evening March 4, 2006. Trying to cheer her desperately ill son, Cyndie suggests, "Maybe we can buy PlayStation 2." Derek replies: "No, Mom. I think we'd better use it to pay the rent."

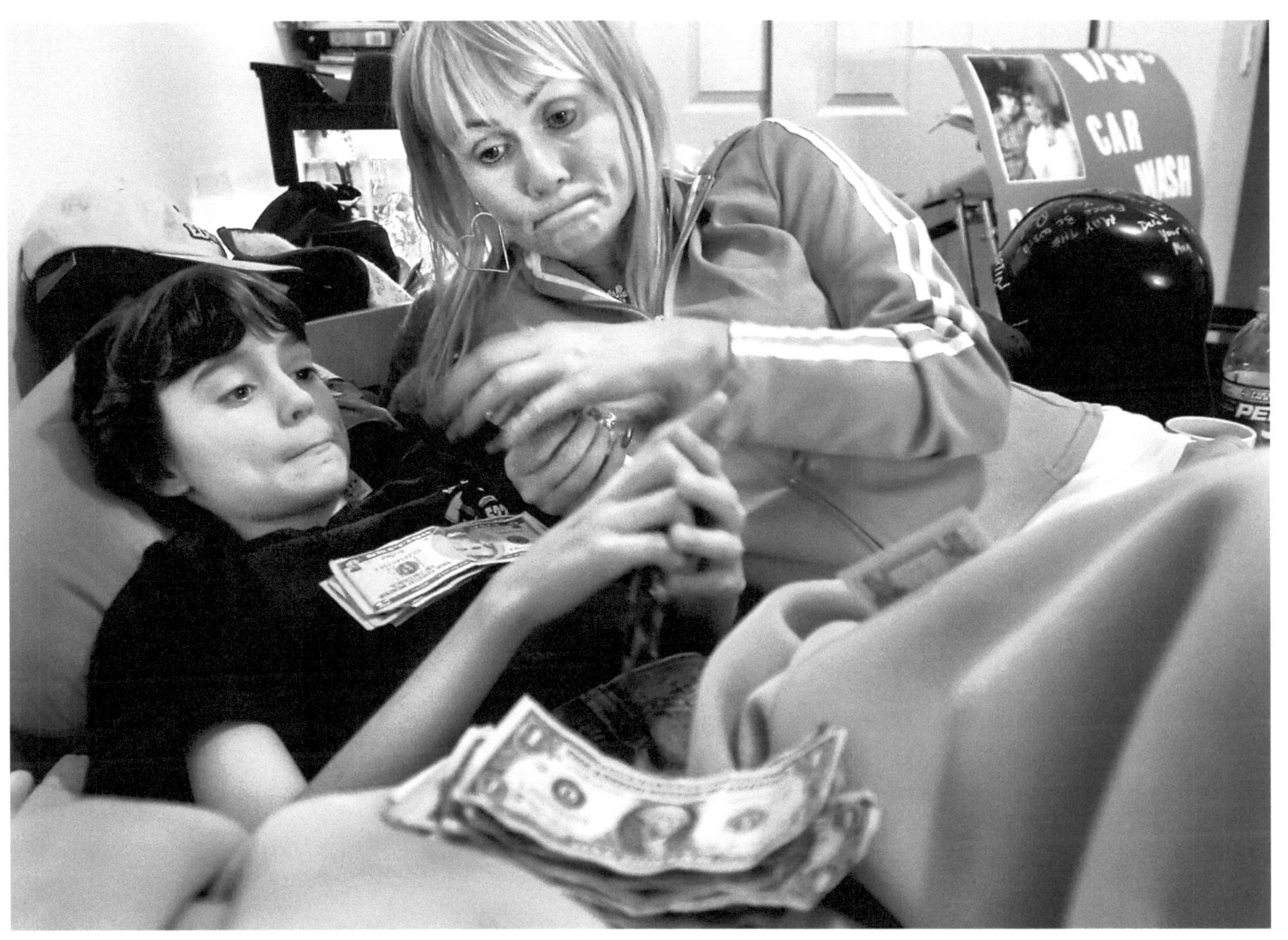
CAR
WASH

Cyndie French always tries to have something at hand to take the sting out of Derek's doctor appointments. On March 8 after undergoing radiation treatment, they make the most of a dollar can of Silly String - and Cyndie then meticulously cleans up every bit of the stuff from the ground. Cyndie is a big fan of the Dollar Store.

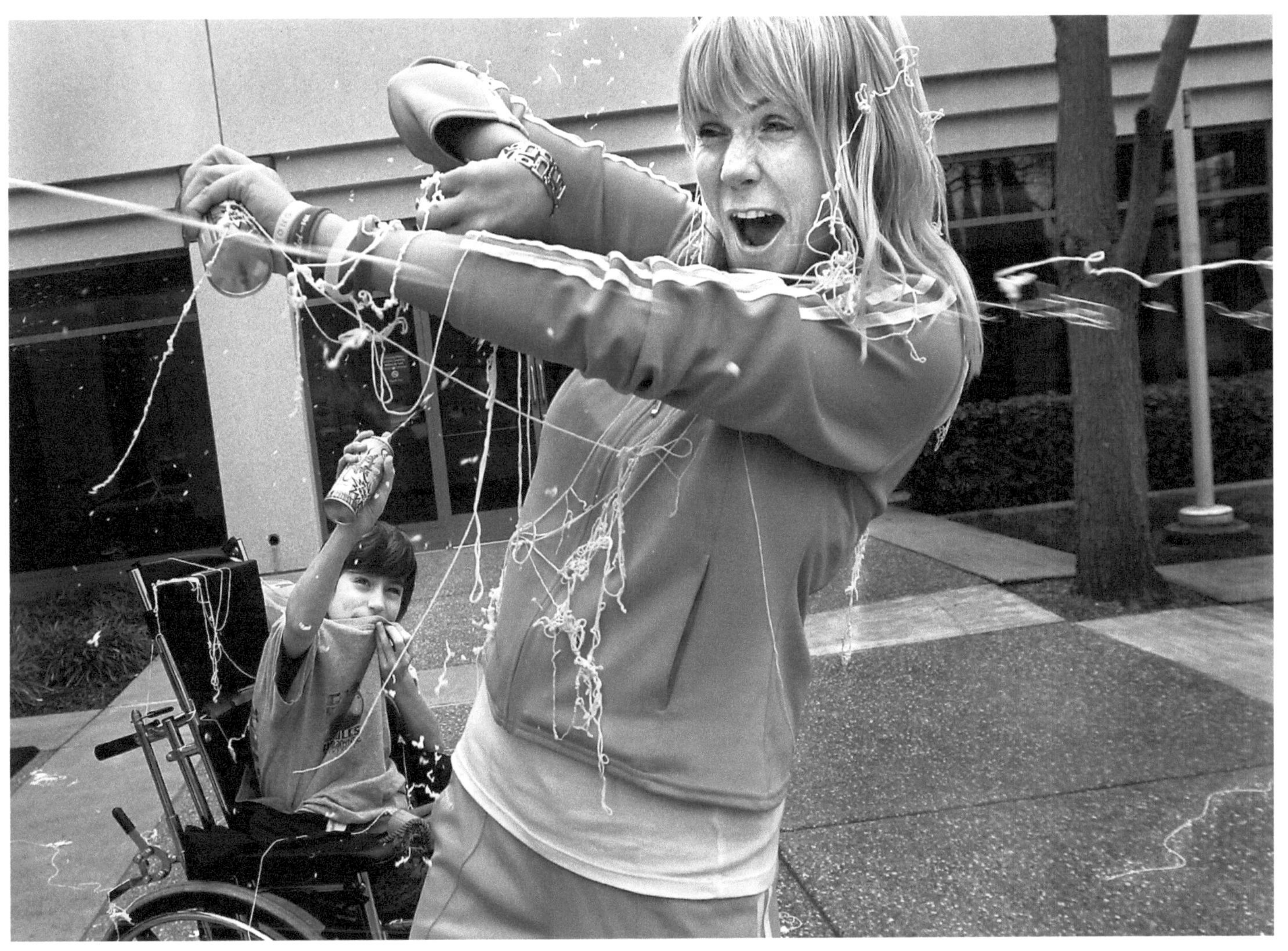

Cyndie French waits for Derek to decide on receiving an emergency radiation treatment for a rapidly spreading tumor at UC Davis Medical Center on April 22, 2006. Derek said, "I'm so confused. It's hard to make a decision. I don't want brain damage." It was his final radiation treatment.

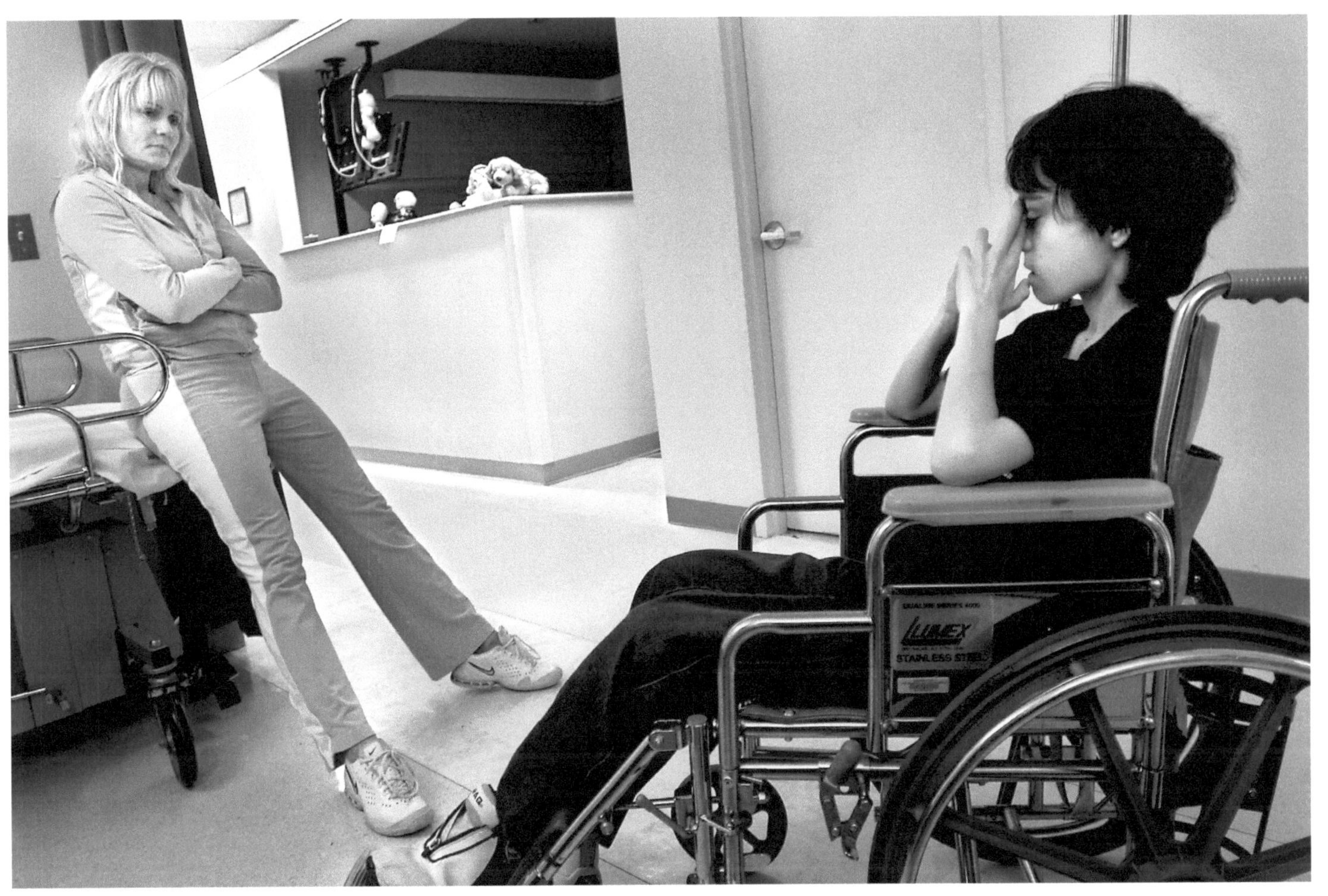
LUMEX
STAINLESS STEEL

Derek is embarrassed and frightened April 10, 2006, by a black eye caused by the cancer's spread behind his left eye. To remind him of the people who love him, his mother has tacked messages above his bed from waitresses at Nick's Diner, his favorite restaurant in West Sacramento.

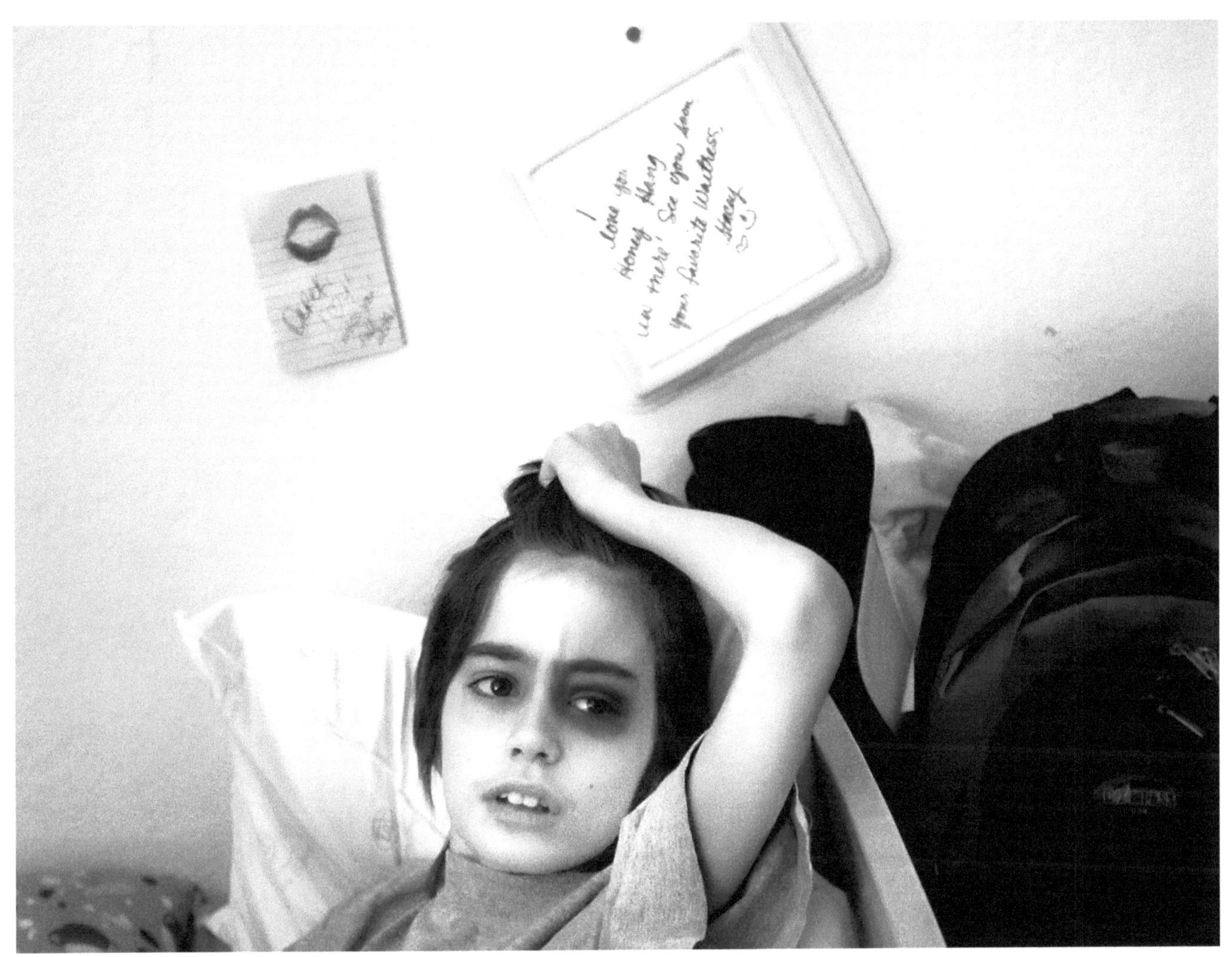

Cyndie French consoles her best friend, Kelly Whysong, left, on April 24, 2006, fearing Derek's time is near. Cyndie wrote a letter to Derek about how brave he's been during his battle with cancer. She reads it to her youngest son repeatedly, hoping he can still understand.

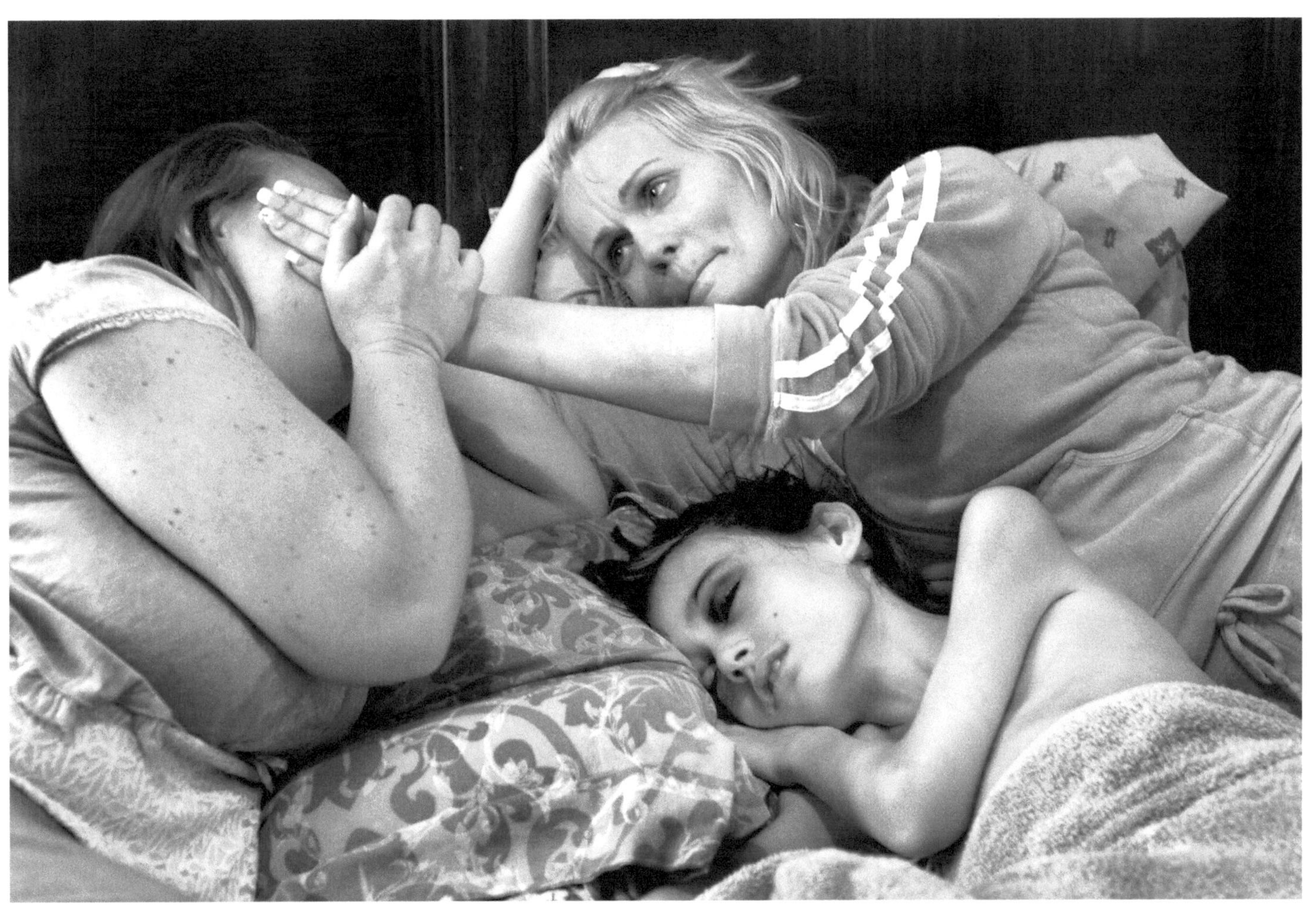

After placing a flower beside her son's head, a sobbing Cyndie drops to the floor on April 25, as her best friend, Kelly Whysong, left, and another friend, Nick Rocha, comfort her. Derek is too weak to acknowledge his mother's presence as she keeps a 24-hour vigil by his bed.

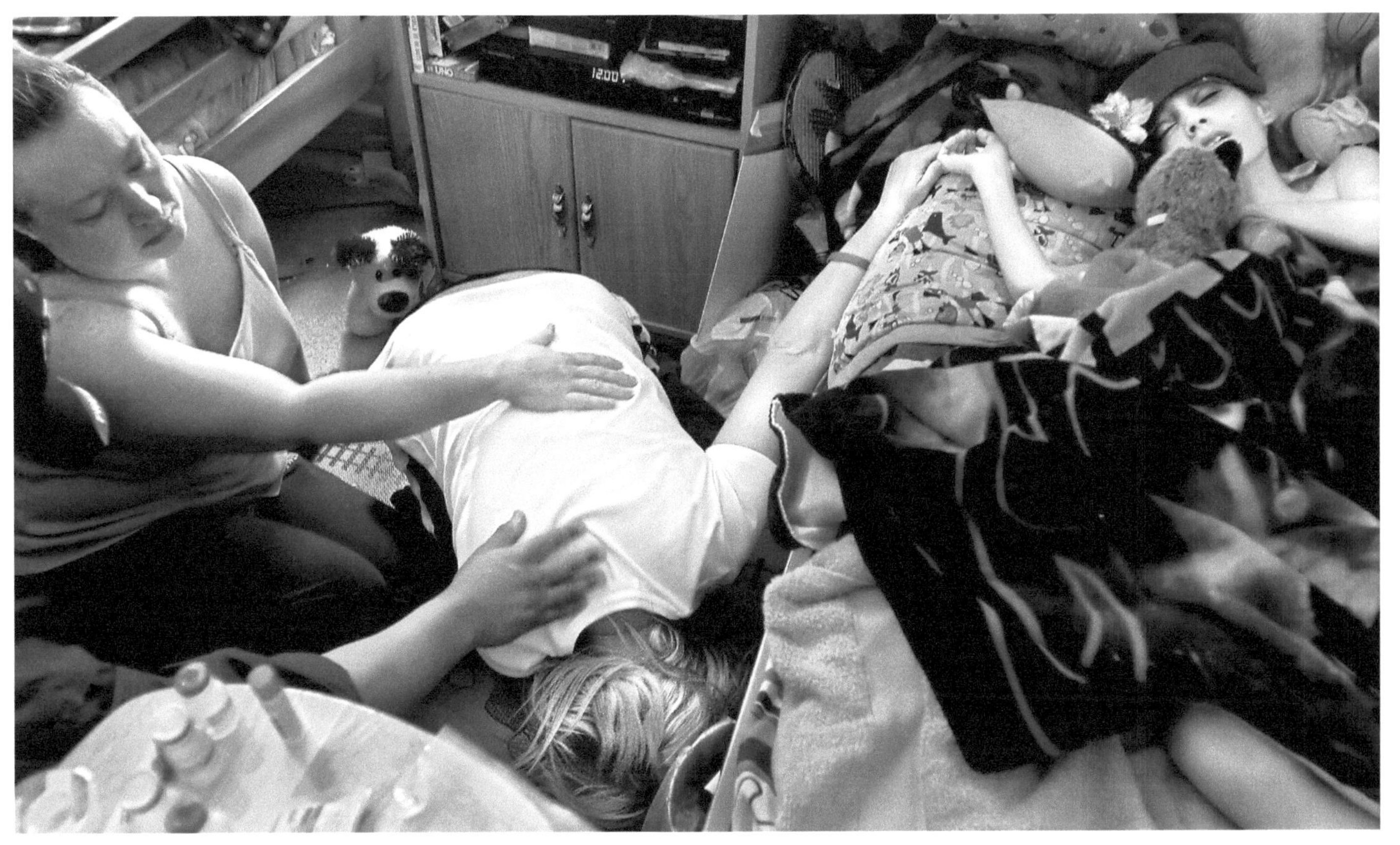
UNO
12:00

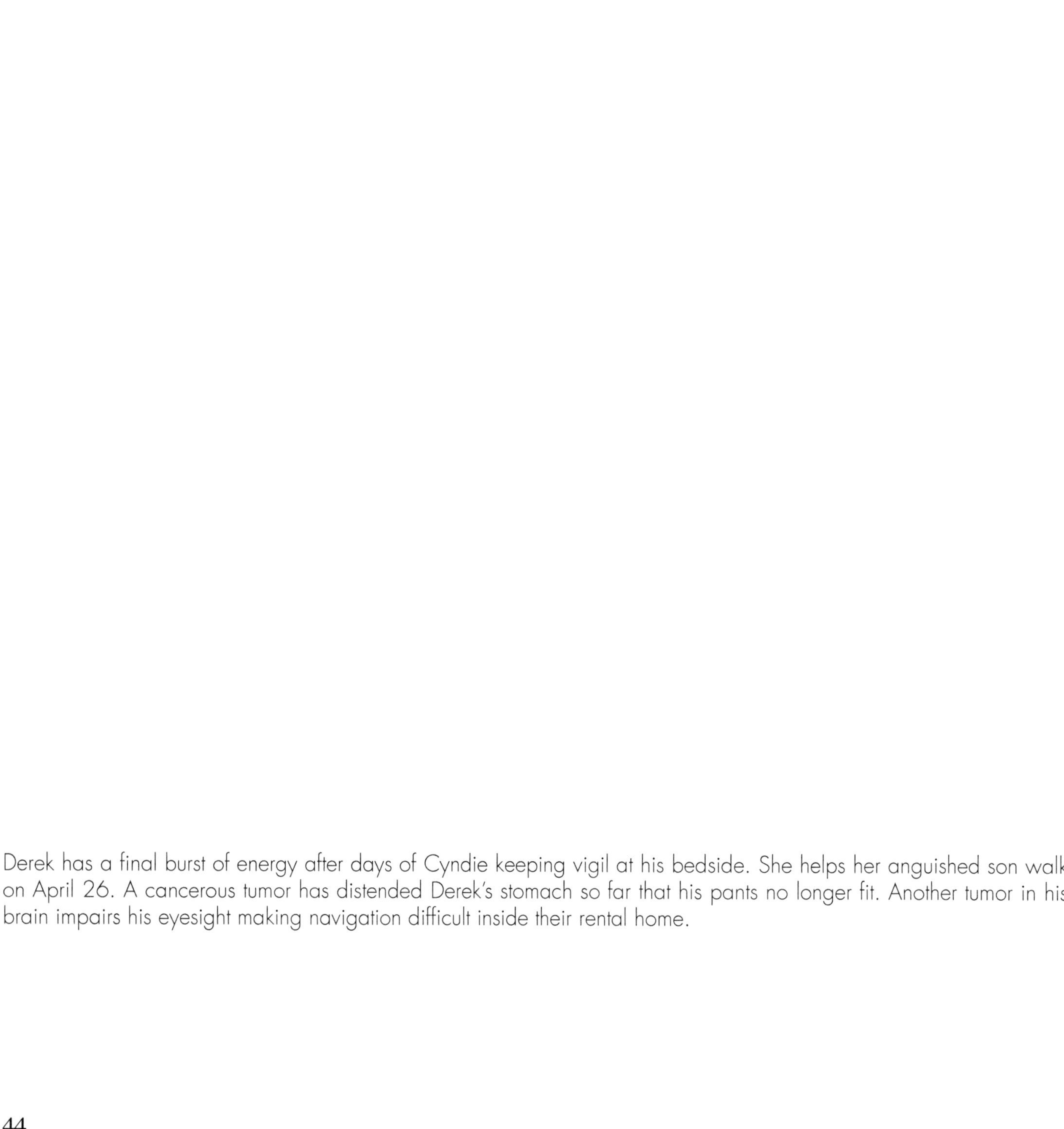

Derek has a final burst of energy after days of Cyndie keeping vigil at his bedside. She helps her anguished son walk on April 26. A cancerous tumor has distended Derek's stomach so far that his pants no longer fit. Another tumor in his brain impairs his eyesight making navigation difficult inside their rental home.

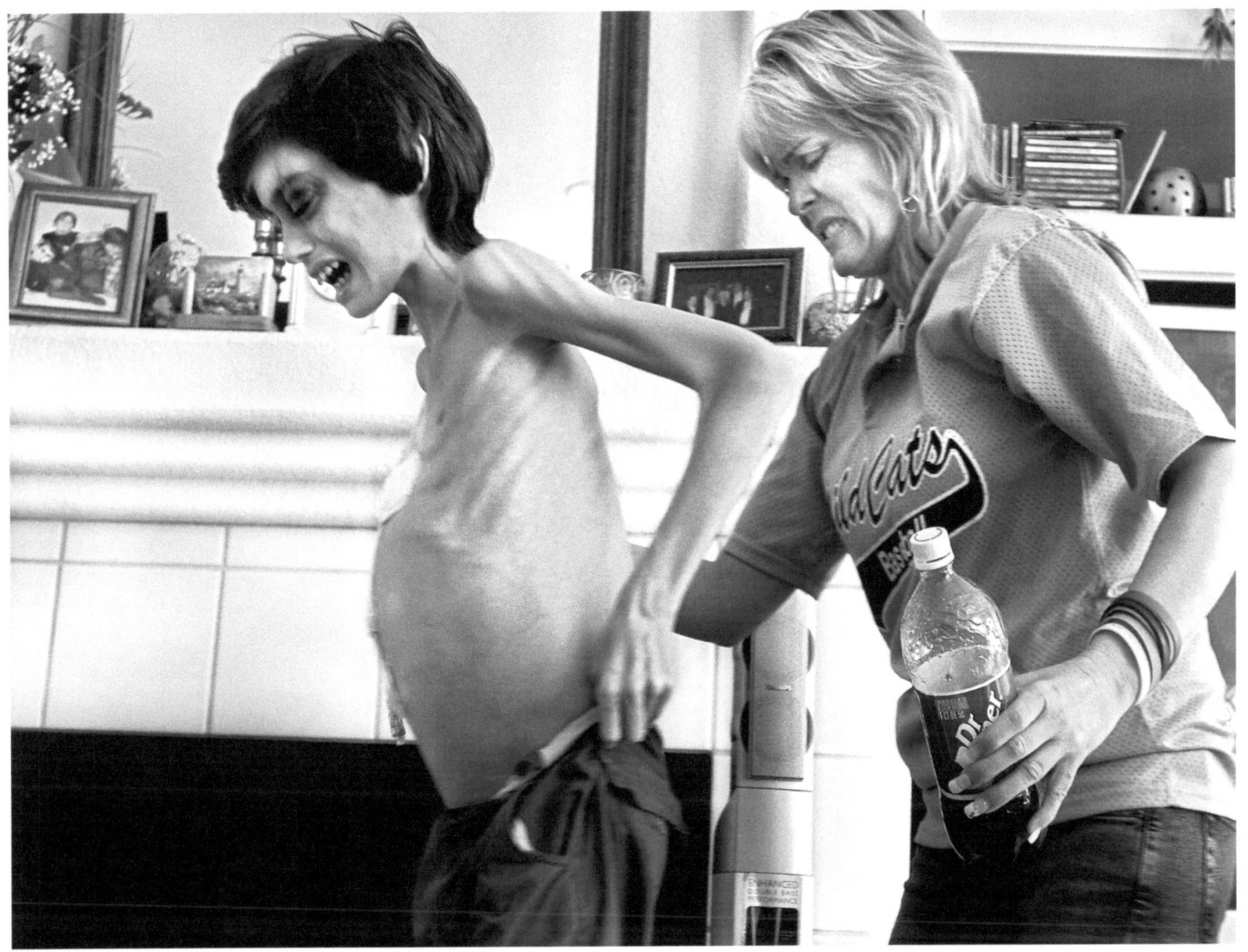

Derek refuses to take pain medications because he fears further damage to his organs. He rages at his mother on April 28, blaming her for not making him healthier. "You have to calm down and help me help you," Cyndie says.

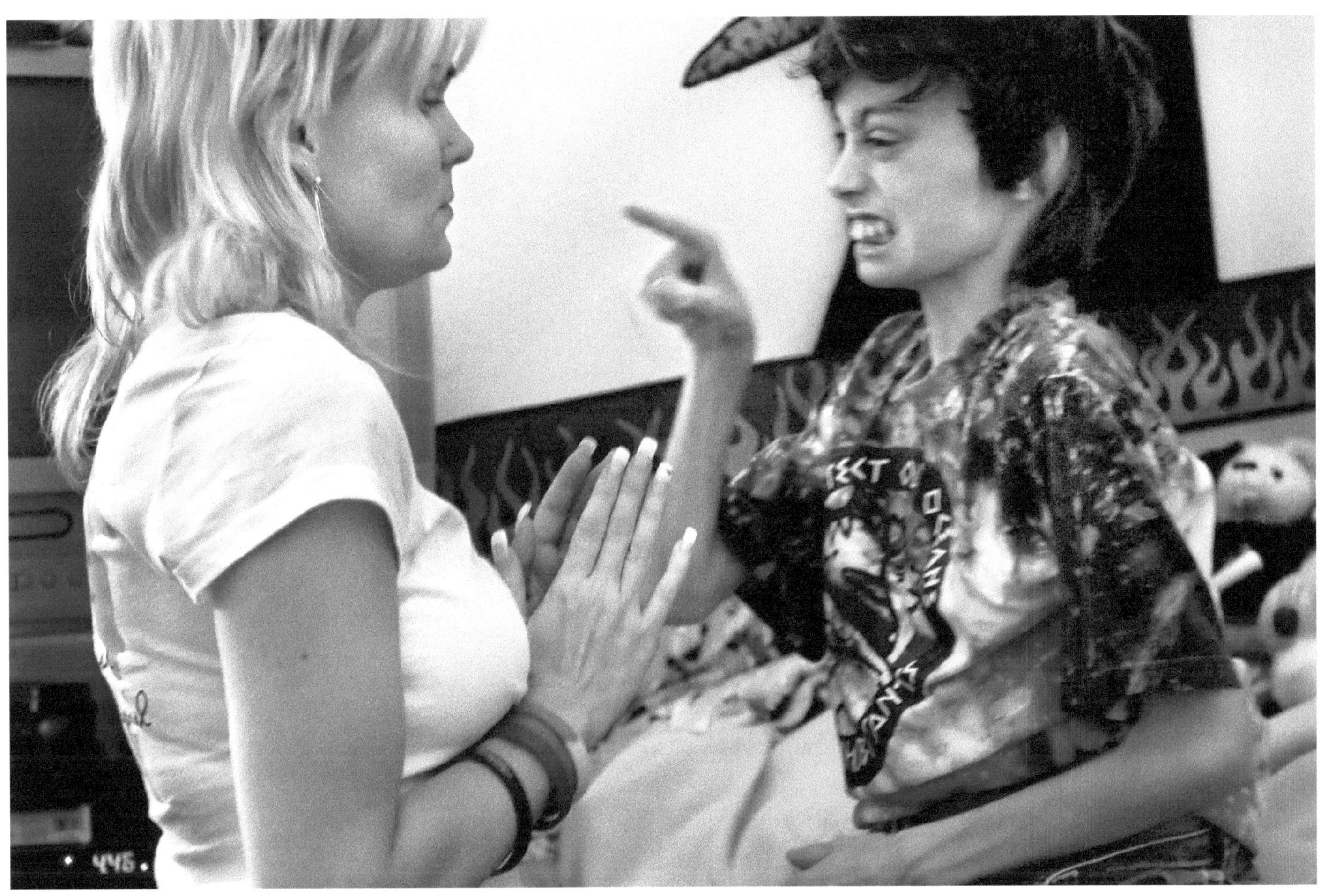

On May 1, after days of little sleep while caring for Derek, Cyndie French confronts longtime family friend "grandpa" Patrick Degnan, about whether he'll be able to help with rent and funeral expenses as Derek is caught in the middle. Cyndie hopes to set up a non-profit organization so families don't have to endure the same financial struggle and chaos they have experienced. "I just wish that some of the percentage of money that goes to cancer research can be diverted to families going through this because many people will never benefit from the research," says Cyndie.

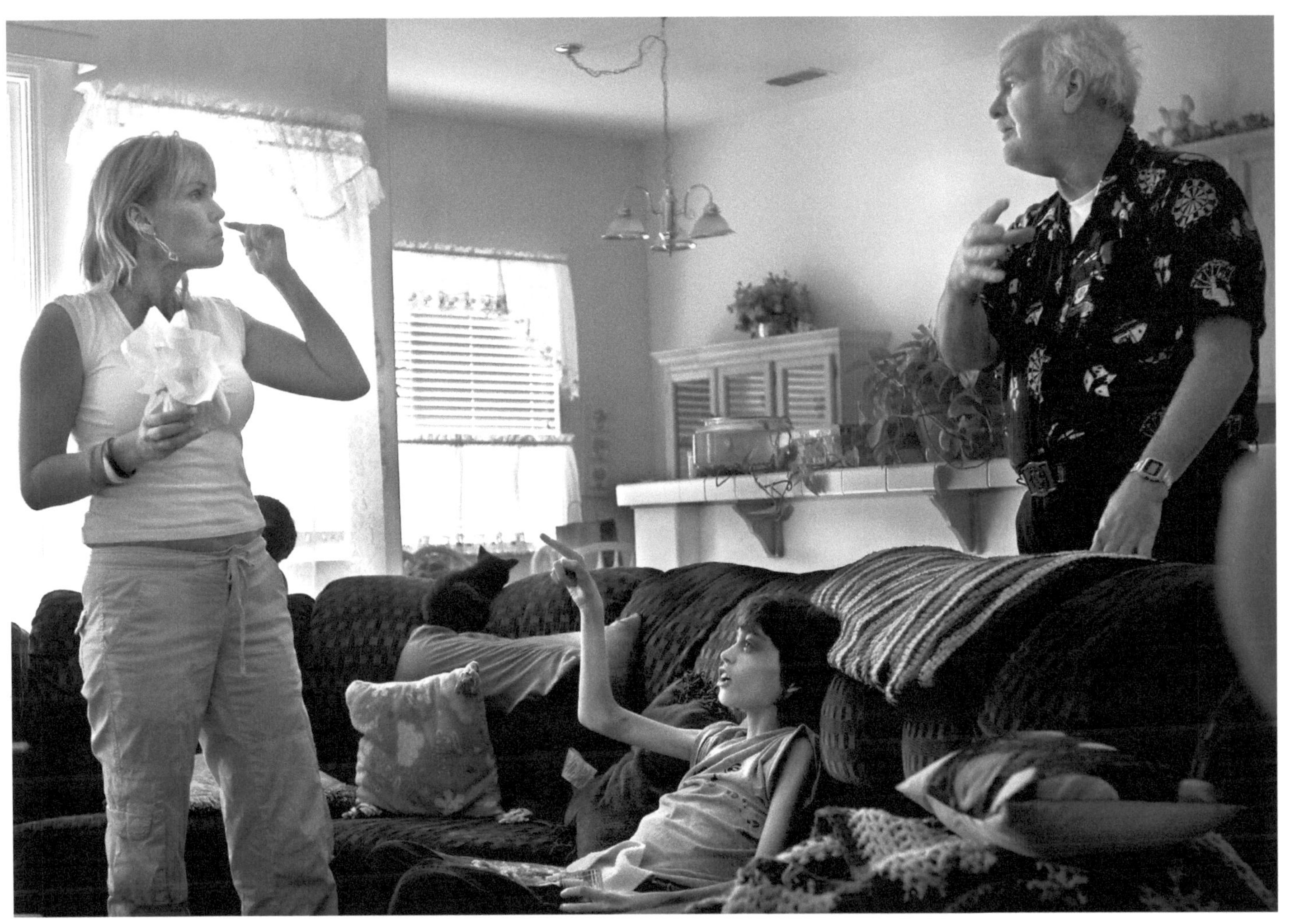

Cyndie French gives Derek medicine May 2, 2006, while he takes a bath, one of the things he still enjoys since tumors have enlarged his stomach. "We have had many long chats while he is in the tub," says Cyndie, who sometimes lights candles and turns on music to soothe her son. Moments earlier, Derek told her, "Mommy, you are the greatest."

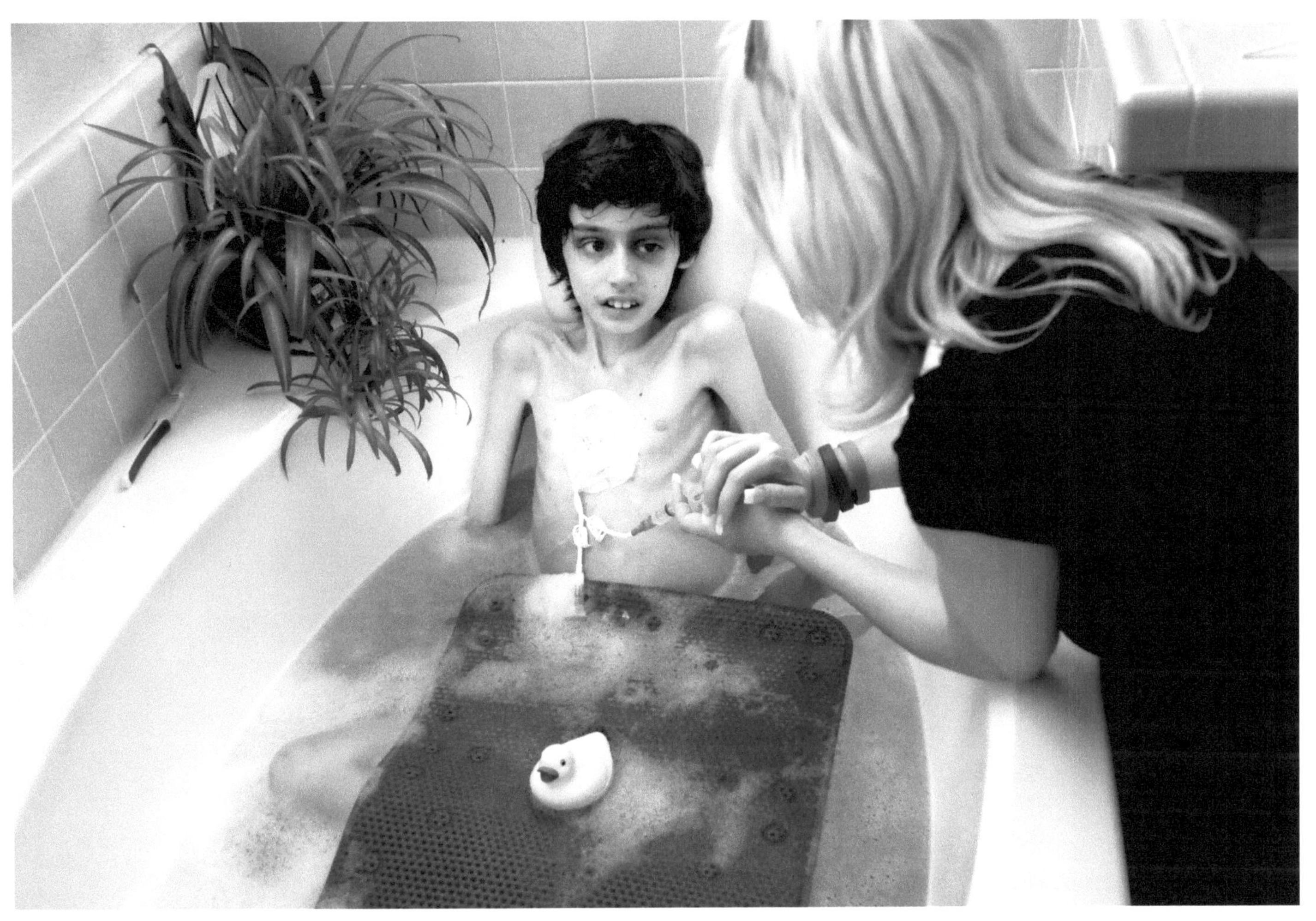

Derek kisses his mom at the Relay for Life benefit, as his 6-year-old sister, Brianna, stands by. Wanting to contribute something to the cause and to "give back," Cyndie recruited volunteers for the benefit. Before the race, Cyndie speaks to the crowd about her pride in her son's bravery during his battle with cancer.

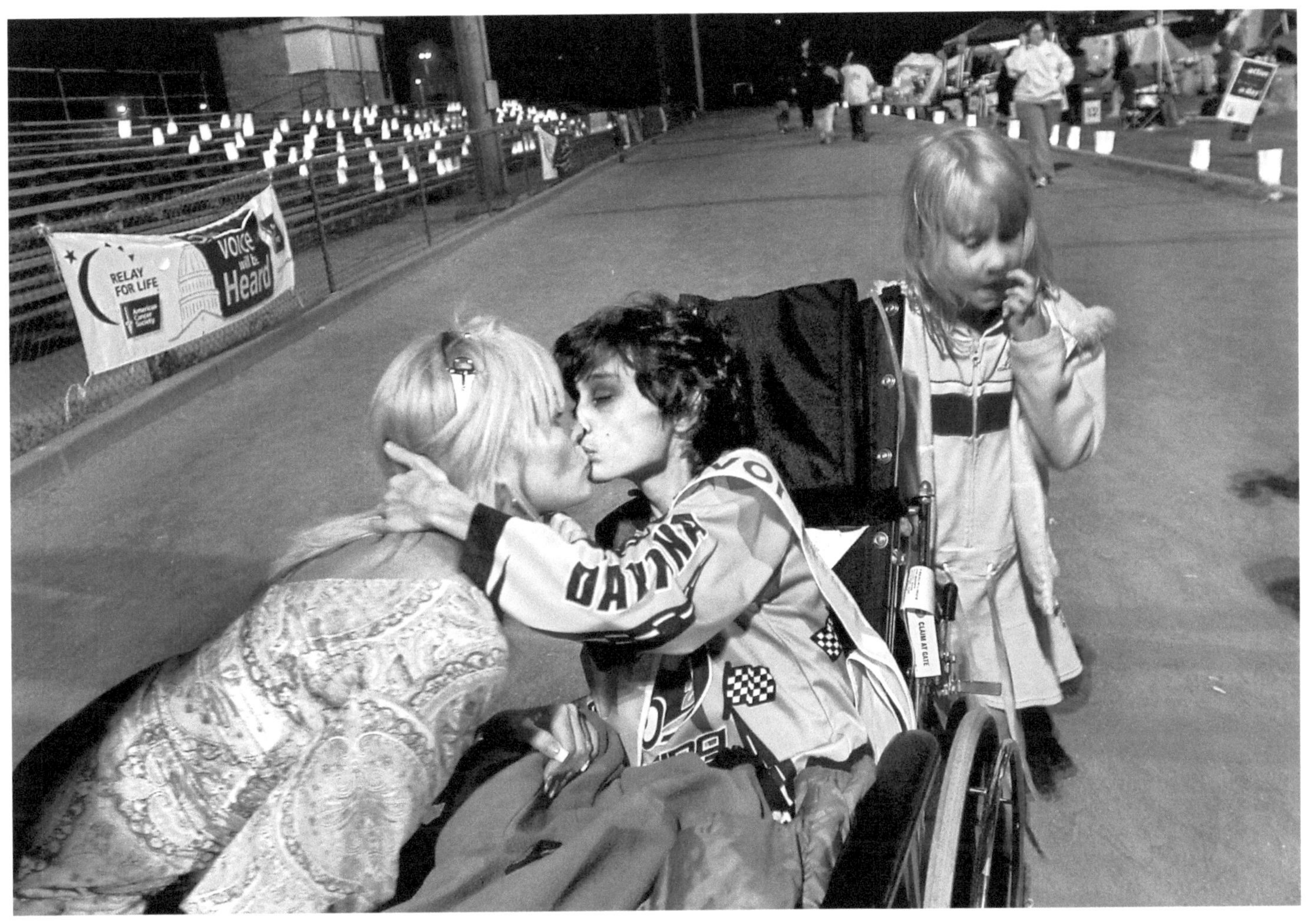
RELAY FOR LIFE
Voice will be Heard
CLAIM AT GATE

Cyndie French holds Derek on May 8, 2006. He is on medication that hinders his speech and keeps him awake at night. Except for a few minutes while hospice nurses are with him, Cyndie spends nearly every moment of the day at his side. "I was exhausted beyond belief but I had to do this. He would call my name and always expects me to be there," Cyndie said.

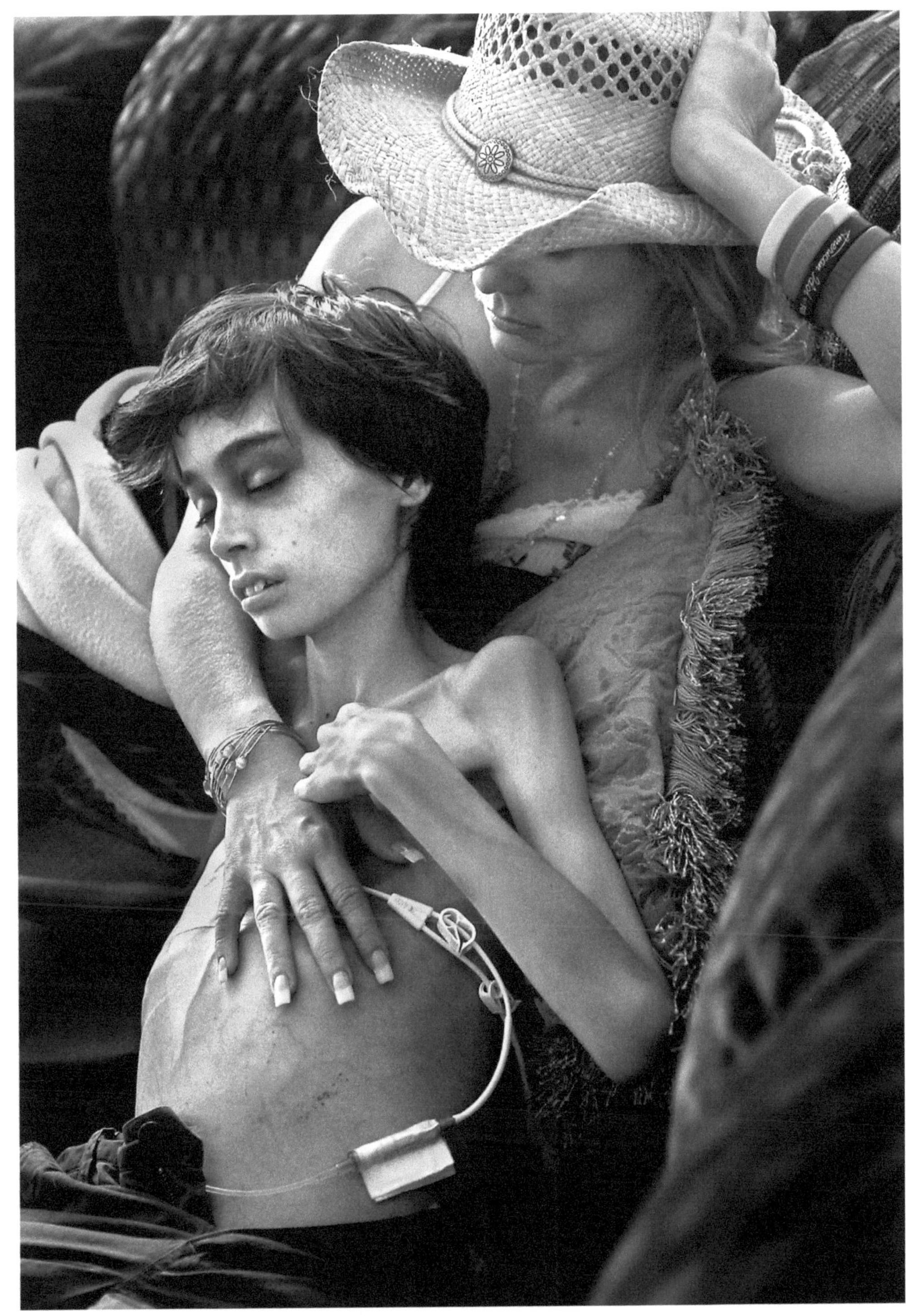

In an effort to get Derek outside, Cyndie French wheels him through the front door passing by artwork and cards given to her son by classmates at Bridgeway Island Elementary School. "Just like a newborn, he needs to get out and get some air," she says. It was his last trip outdoors.

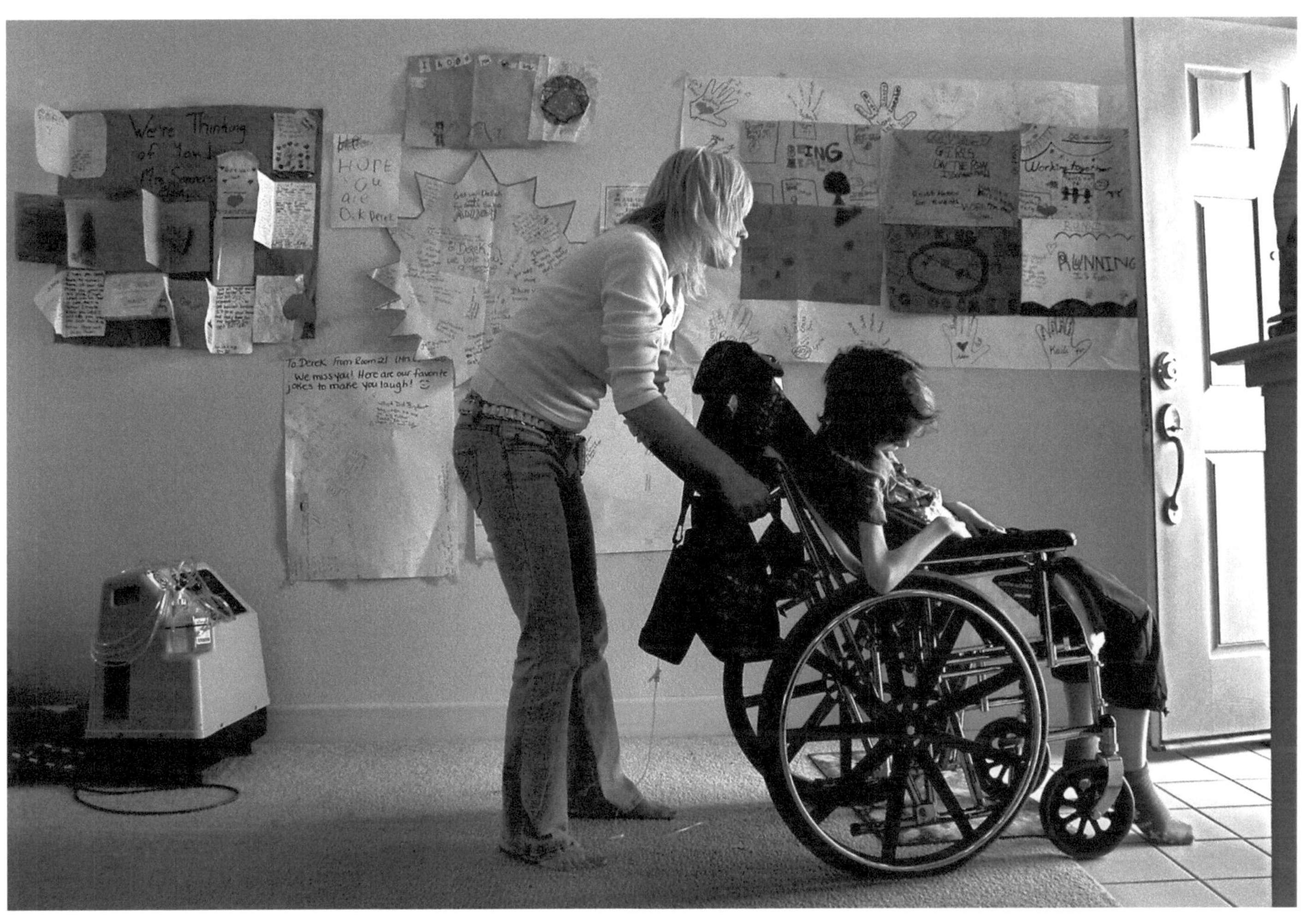
We're Thinking
HOPE
BEING
RUNNING
To Derek From Room 21
We miss you! Here are our favorite jokes to make you laugh!
Working together

Cyndie French fights her emotions May 10, 2006, as she prepares to flush out Derek's catheter with saline solution before hospice nurse Sue Kirkpatrick, left, administers a sedative that will give the 11-year-old a peaceful death. "I know in my heart I've done everything I can," Cyndie says.

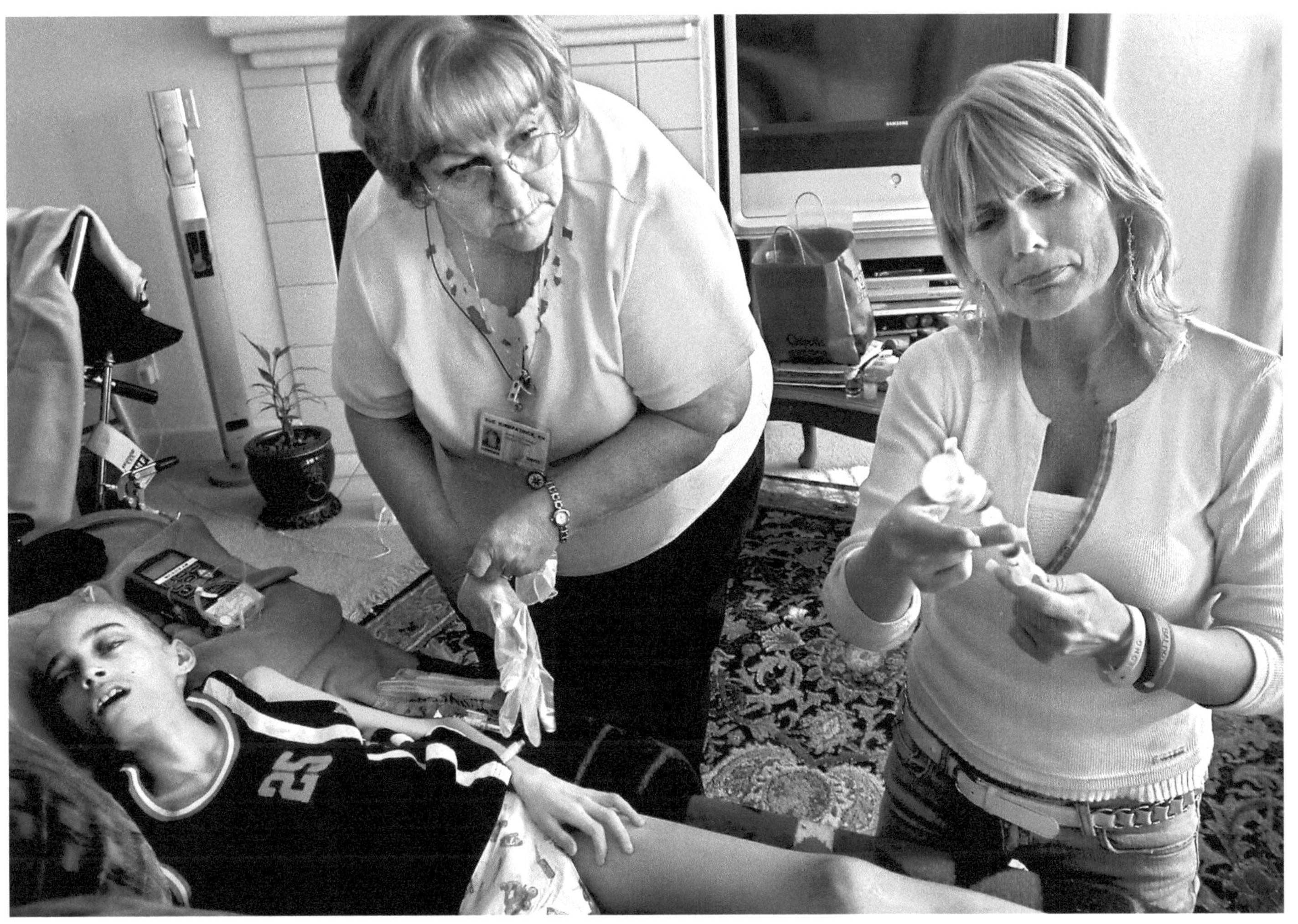
25

Surrounded by friends and relatives, Cyndie French kisses Derek's head as she rocks him in a rocking chair after hospice nurse Sue Kirkpatrick, left, administered a sedative May 10, 2006. Cyndie sings,"You are my sunshine my only sunshine."

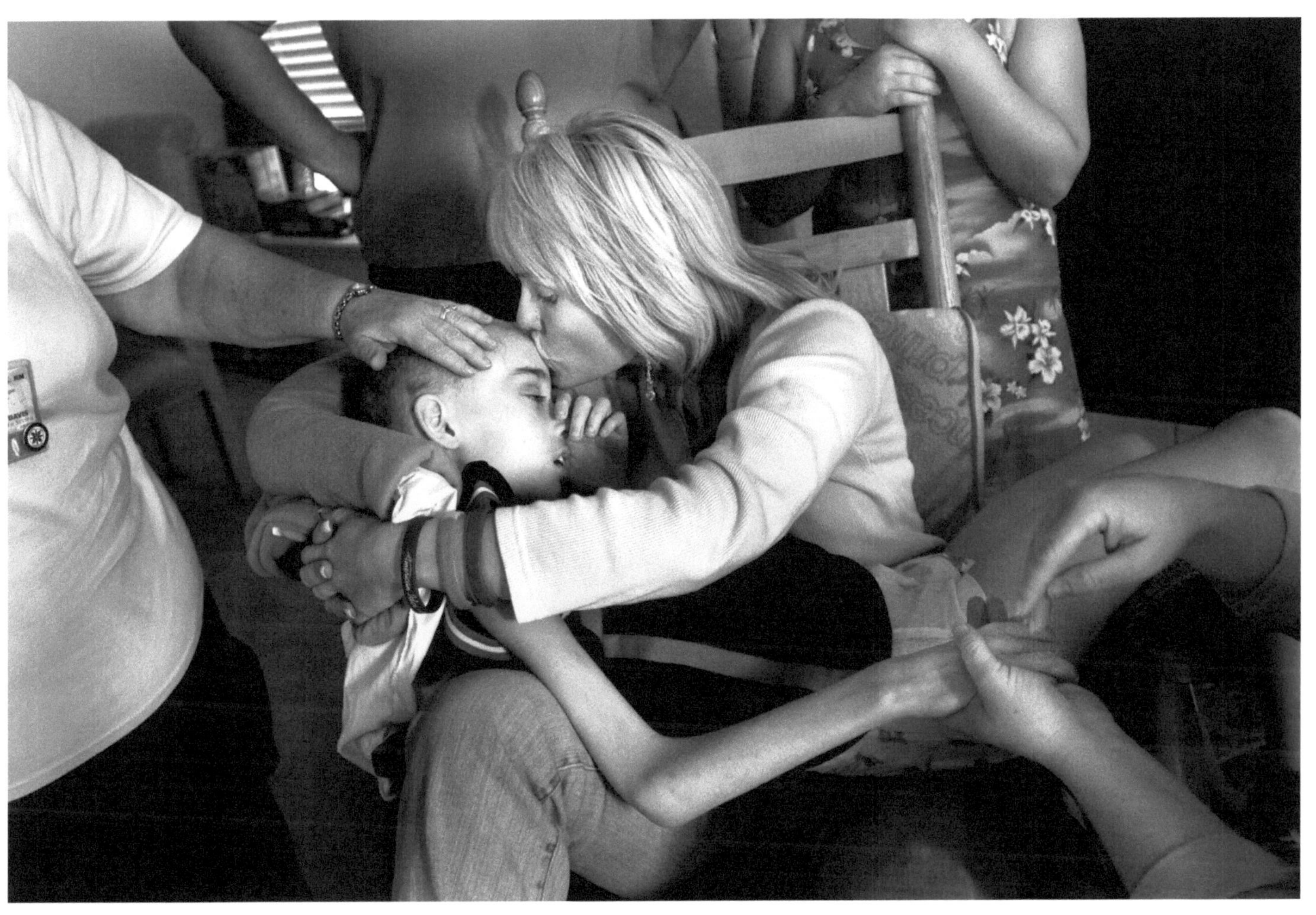

Cyndie French tearfully rocks her dying son Derek , 11, as the song, "Because We Believe," plays. Cyndie sings along with Andrea Bocelli in a whispery voice. "Once in every life/There comes a time/We walk out all alone/And into the light..." From left, family friends Ashley Berger, Amy Morgan and Kelly Whysong offer comfort as Cyndie tells Derek, "It's OK, baby. I love you, little man. I love you, brave boy. I love you. I love you." Derek died soon after in his mother's arms on May 10, 2006.

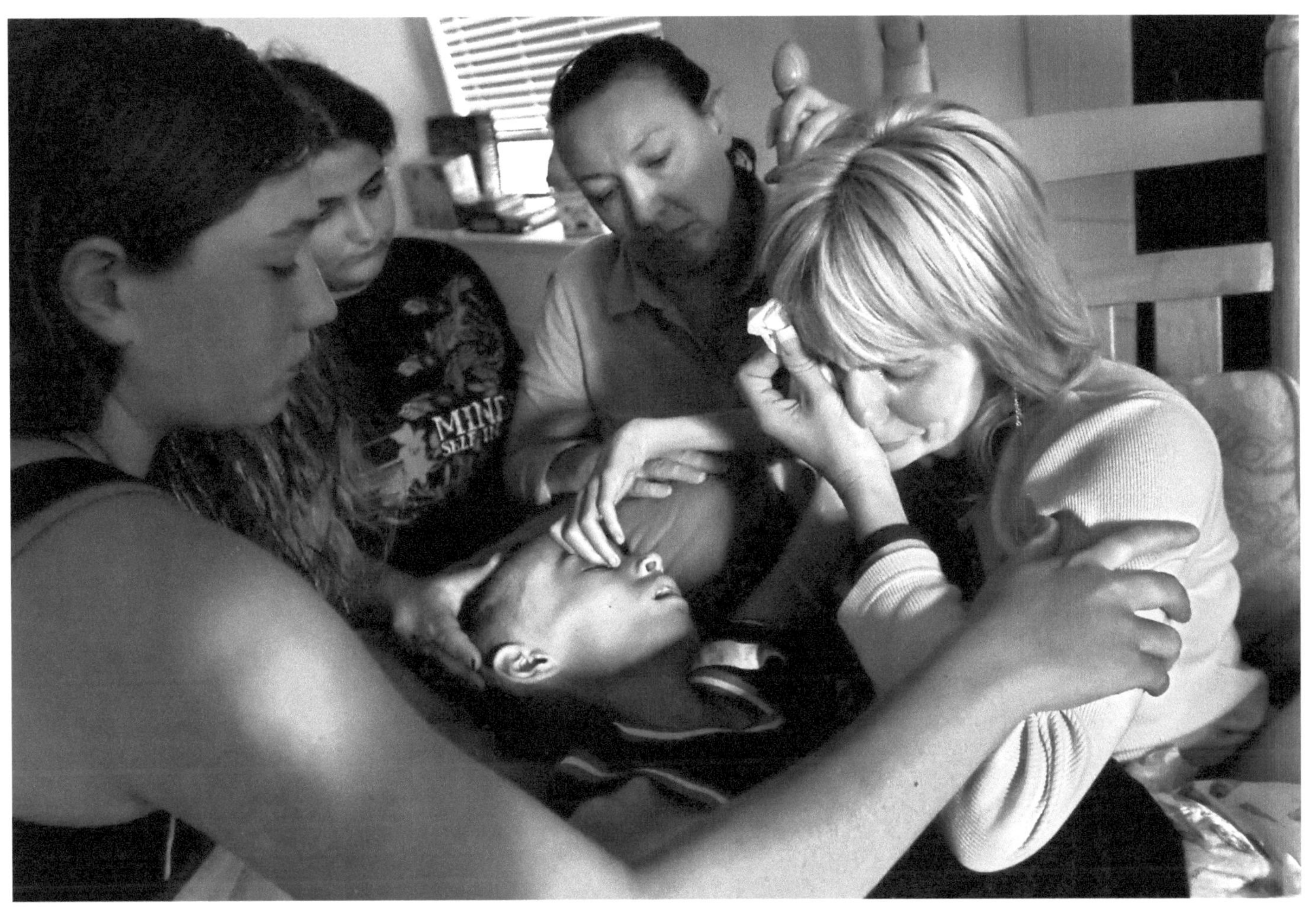

Cyndie French leads Derek's casket to burial with assistance from her sons Anthony Moffe, foreground, Micah Moffe, opposite him, and Vincent Morris, who is not visible, as well as several friends. "I will forever carry your memory in my heart and remind others to give of their time, energy and support to other families like ours," Cyndie says at the funeral. Derek was buried in Mount Vernon Memorial Park in Fair Oaks, California, on May 19, 2006.

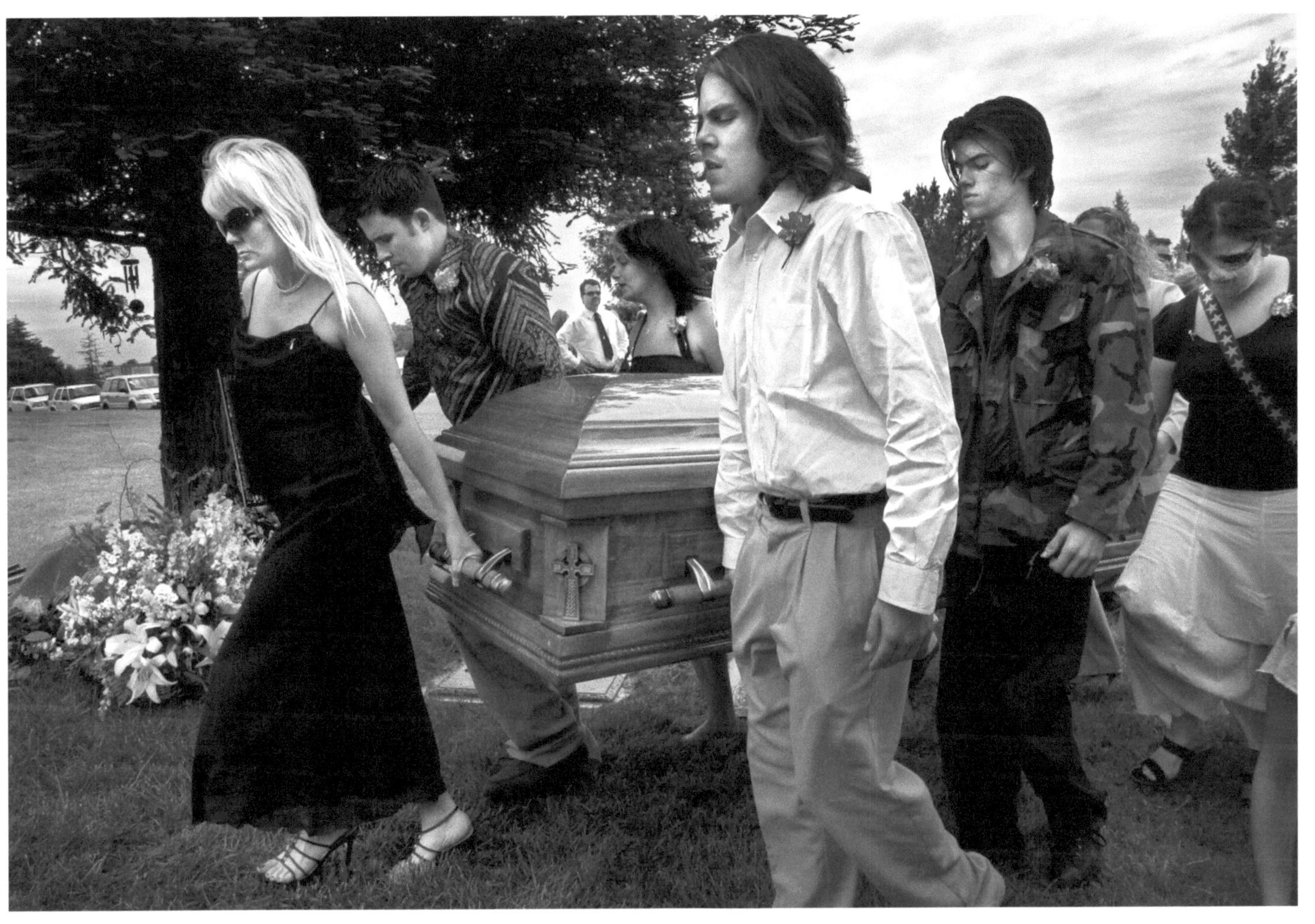

selected photographs

THE BIRDS: In a scene reminiscent of Alfred Hitchcock's famous tale, "The Birds," hundreds of thousands of starlings and grackles fly over rural Woodford County field in Illinois, November 12, 1982. Birds' migration behavior is silent, smooth and subtle. Sometimes, when the temperature drops suddenly, birds panic and flock together as shown in this picture. "Before I made the photograph I was almost too afraid to get out of the car, but I did quickly. If I had hesitated I would have missed the moment because the birds were all gone within a few seconds." This photograph was selected for the Book of Days calendar, edited by Fred Woodward, Art Director of Rolling Stone Magazine in 1991.

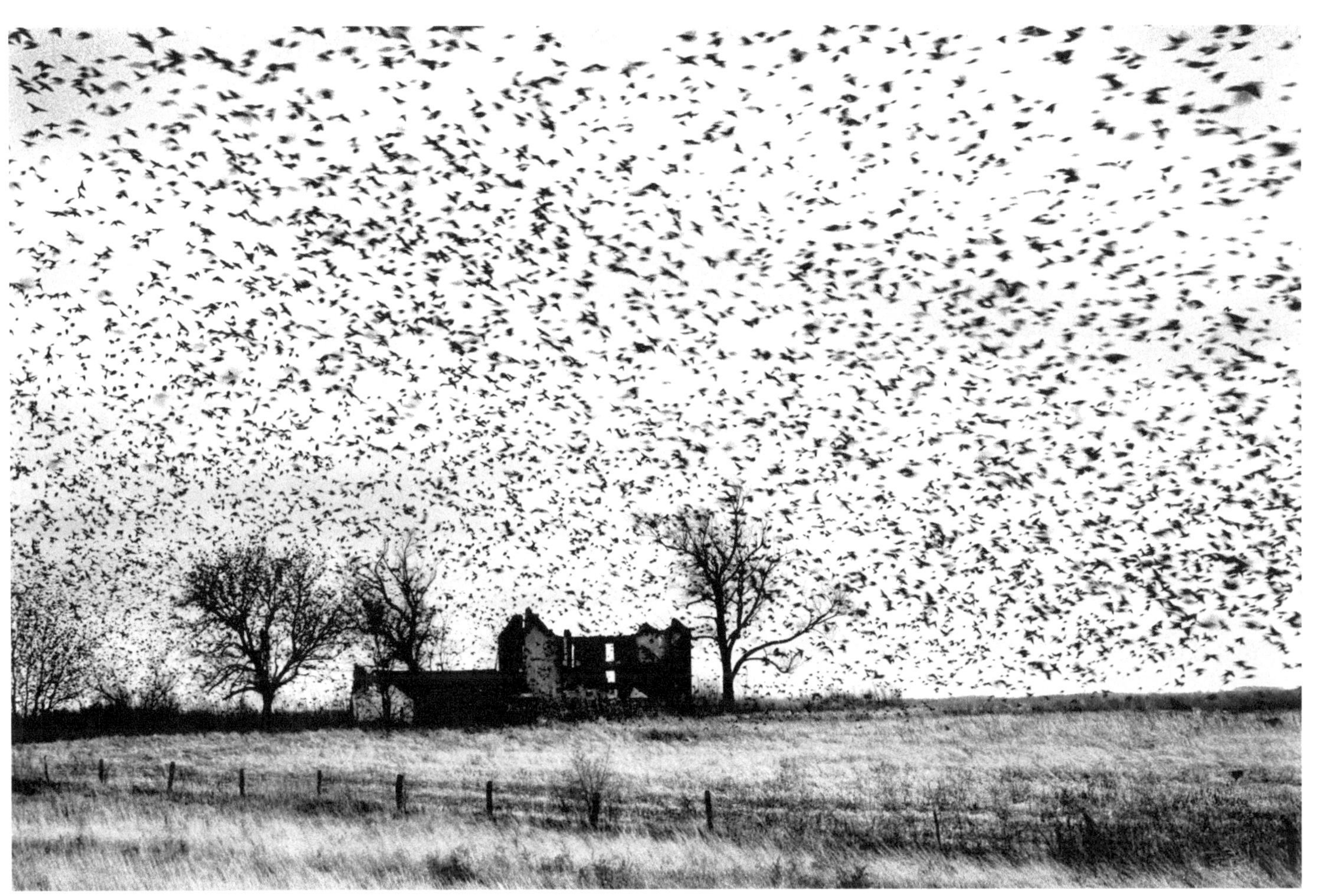

REPEAT CUSTOMER: Charlotte Mook, 83, of West Salem, Oregon gets a perm at Phagan's School of Beauty, where she had worked for 25 years. "I come here more than 12 to 15 times a year and like most everything, but mostly the way they do my hair," said Mook. Photo taken on November 22, 1999.

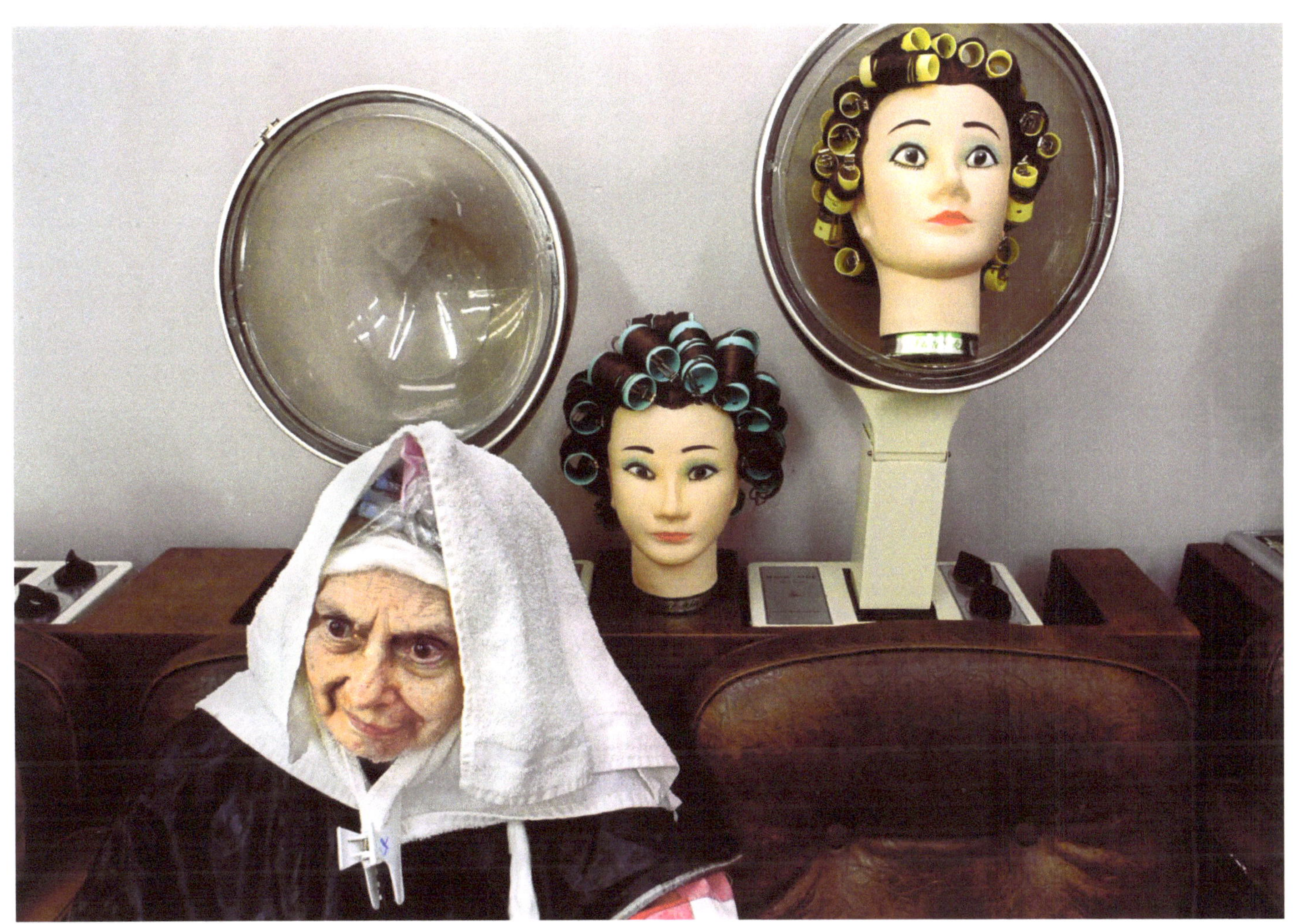

MARDI GRAS RIOTS: Seattle police subdue a man while clearing the streets early Sunday morning after a Mardi Gras celebration turned into a protest. By the end of the week one person died, 69 were injured and several women were sexually assaulted. Chaos erupted late Saturday night, vicious street fights and random hooliganism broke out along side streets and in alleyways leading from Seattle's oldest neighborhood. Police in riot gear shot rubber bullets and tear gas into crowds of unruly revelers in Pioneer Square. Photo taken on February 25, 2001.

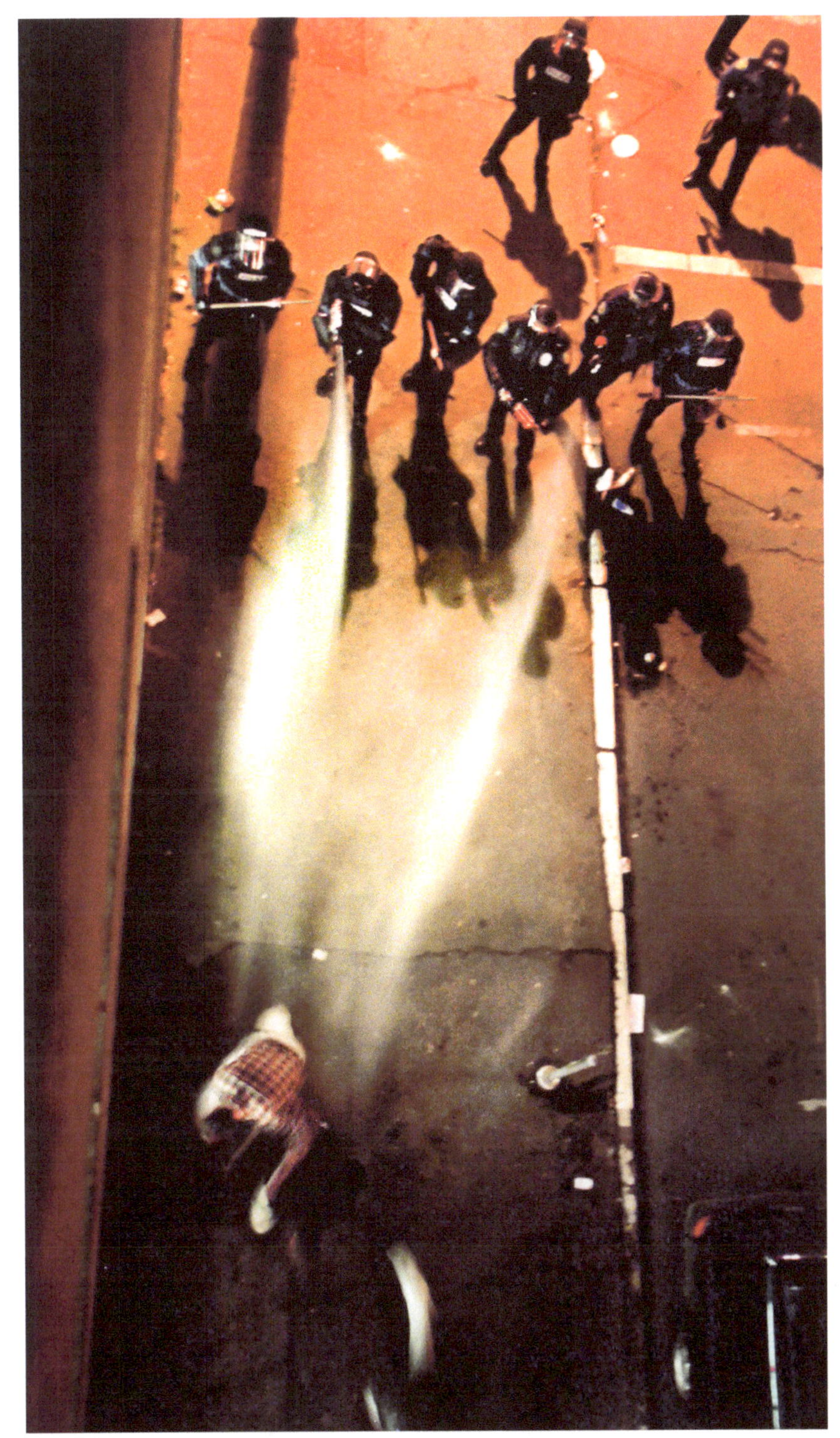

SHADOWED BY NASTY WEATHER: A pedestrian uses an umbrellas a shield against the wind and the rain on the corner of Pike Street and Fourth Avenue in downtown Seattle March 12, 2002.

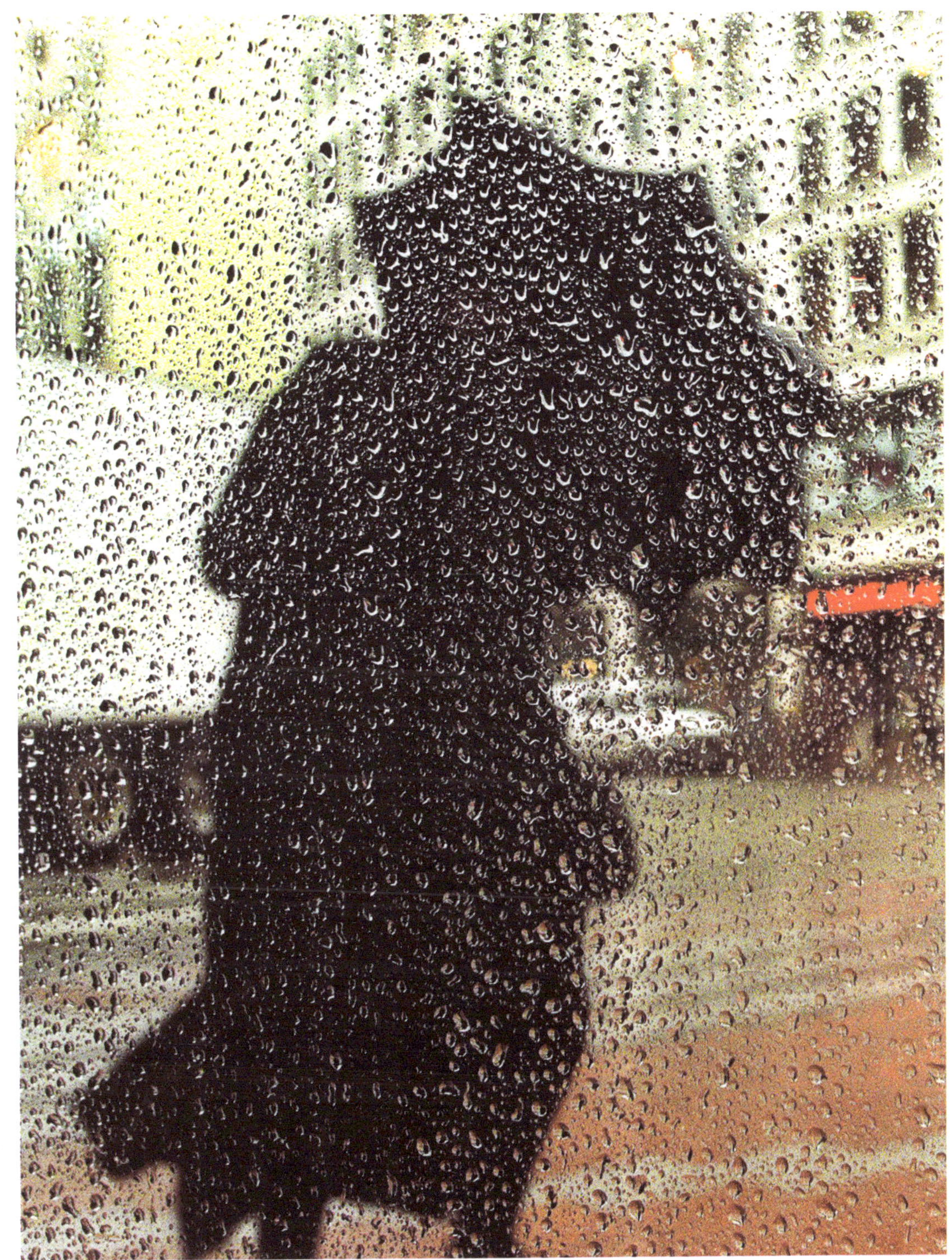

LOW INCOME HOUSING: Lauren Holland, 8, holds her cat as sister Allyson Thomas, 4, reads on the bed in Lauren's tiny bedroom May 2, 2002. Allyson sleeps with her mom on a double bed in the living room of their Seattle apartment. Julia Holland and her children got a break on rent through a public housing levy that was weighted toward low-income people. "I was recording the daily lives of a family that lives in low-income housing in Downtown Seattle. I was trying to show the small bedroom when this juxtaposition of one of the children and her cat appeared. It is not a set-up portrait, it's an actual moment."

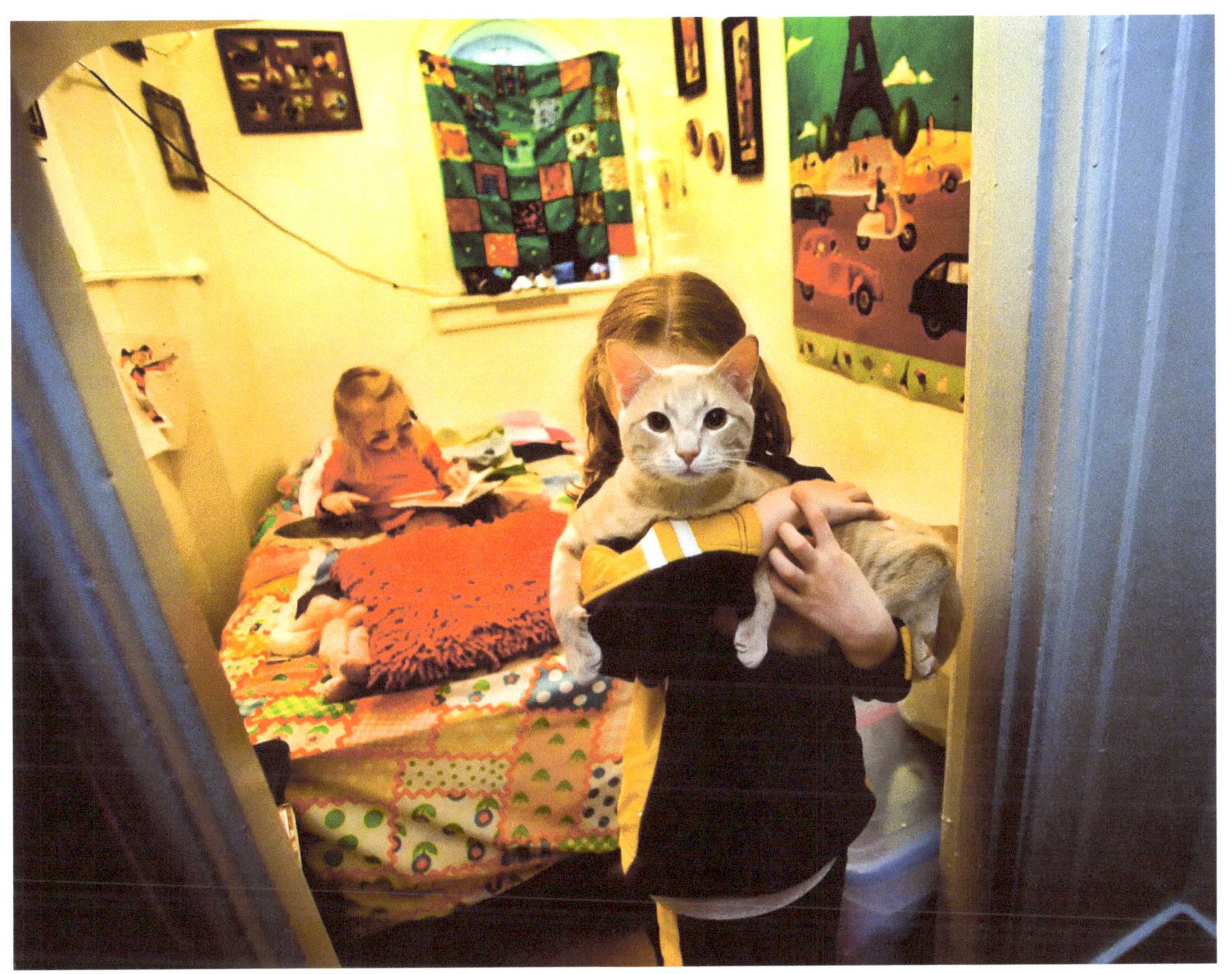

PARENTS MURDERED: Huong Nguyen, 14, center is overcome with grief at the funeral for her parents Hue Nguyen and Loi Thi Ngo who were murdered at their jewelry store on Friday July 25th at their burial at the Sacramento Memorial Lawn cemetery on Friday August 1, 2003. The Nguyen's left behind six children from the ages of 12 to 20. "One of the hardest part of my job is covering personal tragedy...."

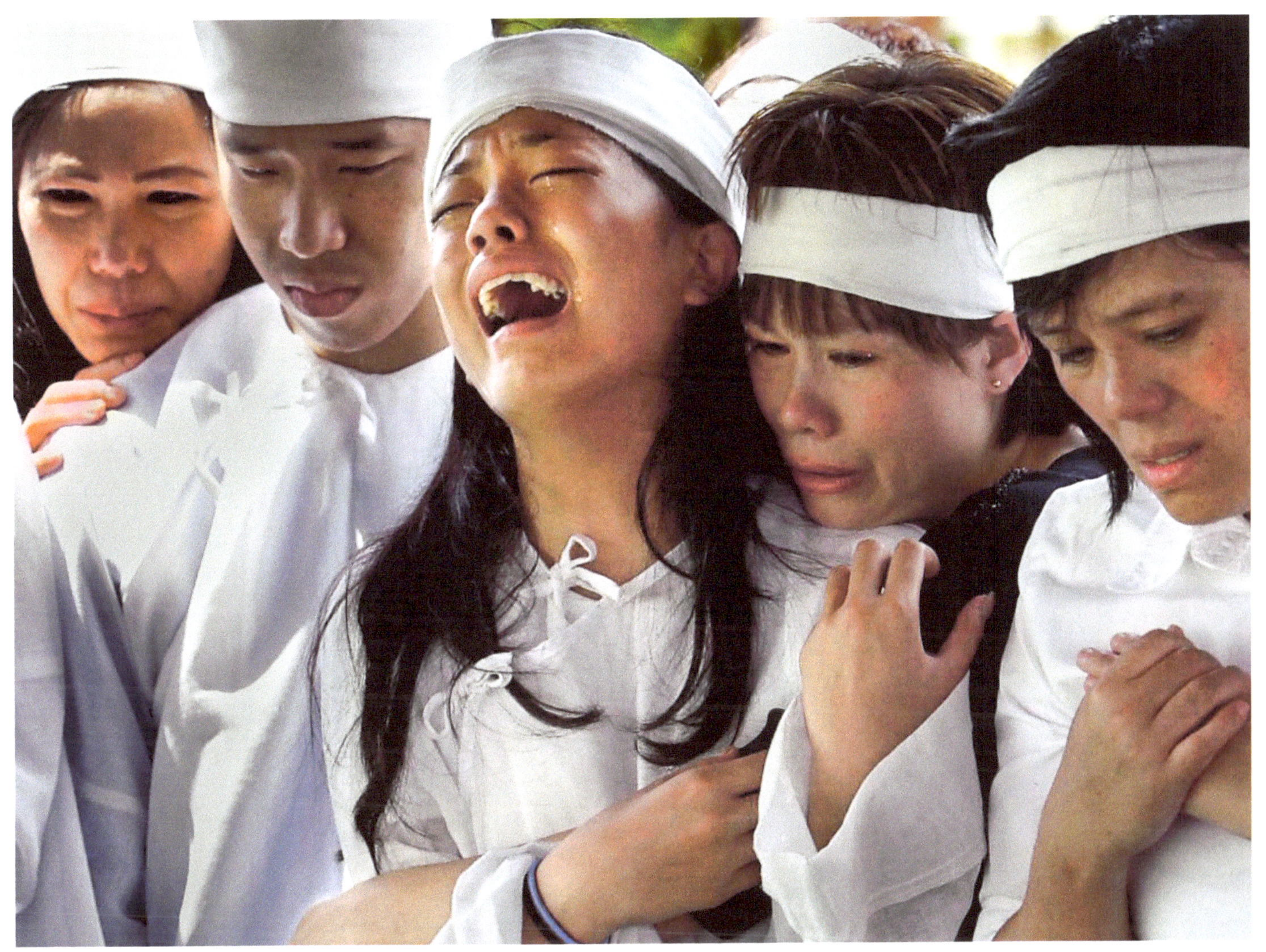

GLOBE TROTTING GENES: Hermenegildo Perez, 87, with his wife Sabina Mendez, 85, has been planting maize in Capulalpam, Mexico since he was 12. He now must buy seed from the government store but says, "The corn from my ancestors is tastier." He says he can tell the difference between the genetically engineered corn - altered to kill insects by producing its own pesticide, which was discovered by UC Berkeley scientists in the hillside fields in 1997 - and their own centuries-old varieties. The villagers were concerned and said they didn't want it because they didn't know the consequences. October 2003.

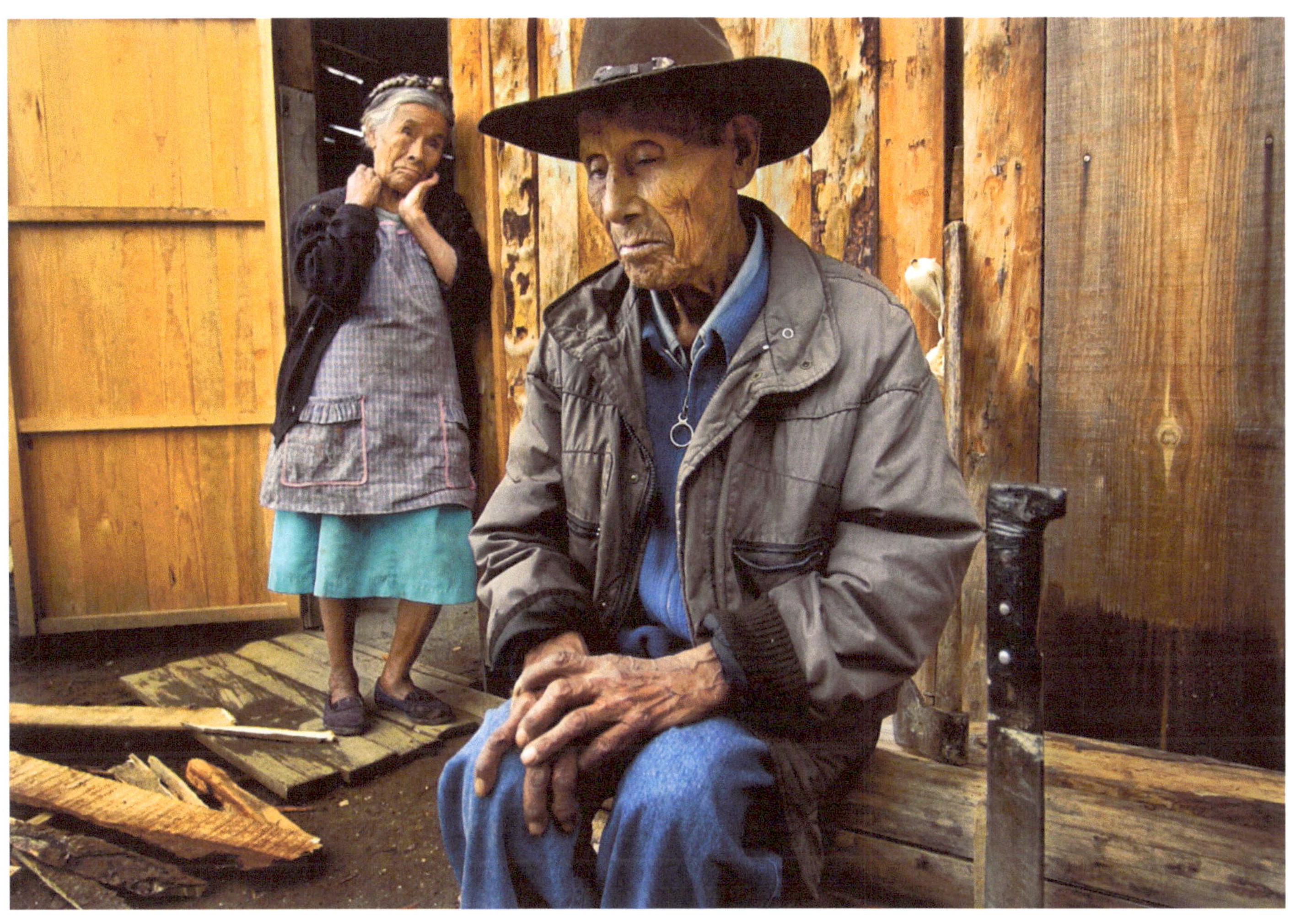

A STRUGGLE TO SURVIVE: Mahamoud Ag Ahmedou, 2, eats a few grains of rice for dinner in a village near the city of Léré in Mali, West Africa March 8, 2004. After helping his mother work burning wood to make coal all day he earned the right to eat. The village chief said those who don't work, don't eat.

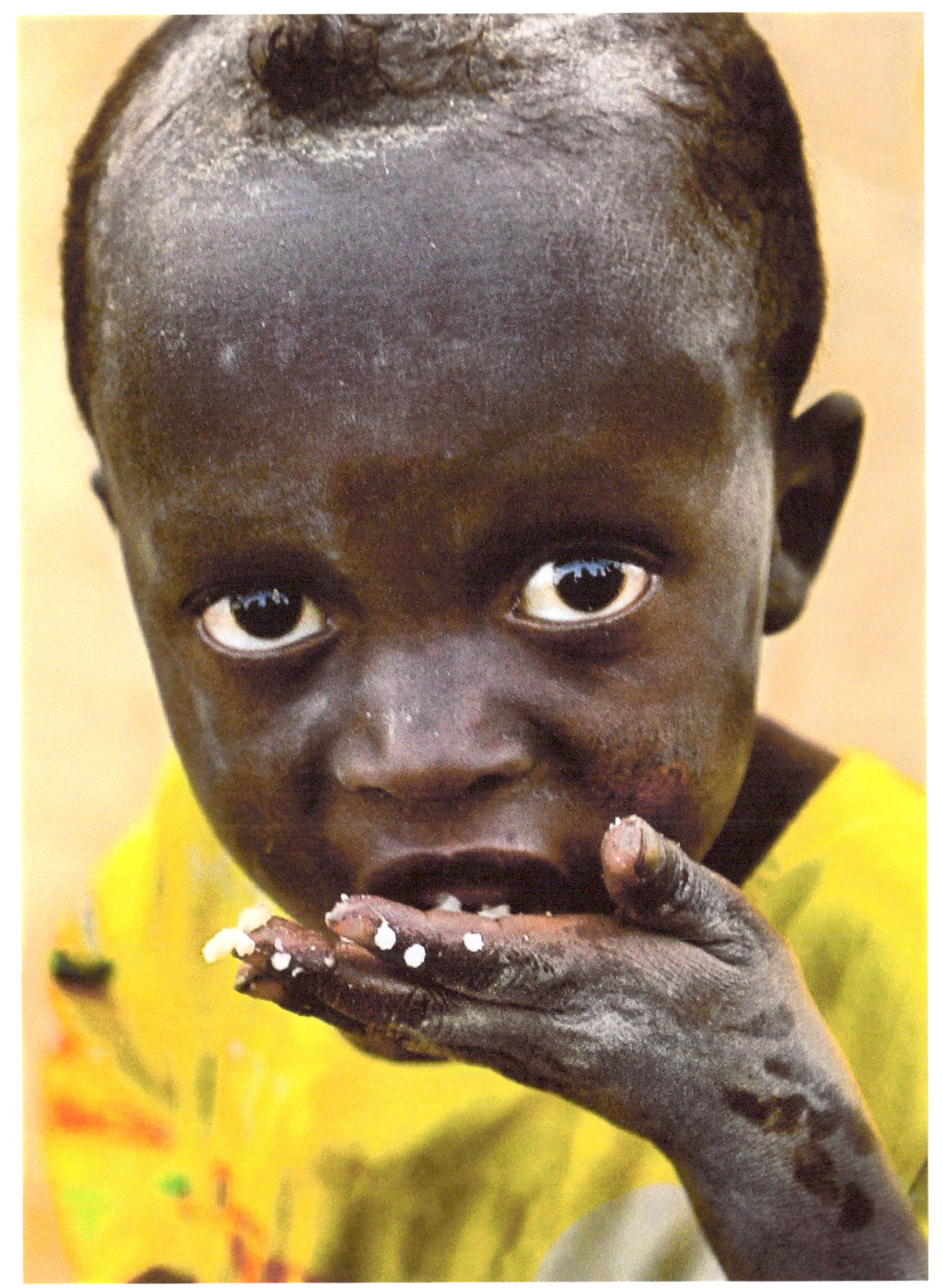

MALARIA MORTALITY: Fadimata Oualet Rhaly, 48, suffers from malaria as Hadsatou Oualet Alkhader, 6, takes care of 3-month-old Mohamed Asseleh Ag Mohamed Ali in the Bela village of Bankore 1-7 Koura March 16, 2004. The average life span in Mali is 49. According to the U.N. Development program, Mali has the highest childhood mortality rate from malaria in the world—2,046 per 100,000 in the year 2000.

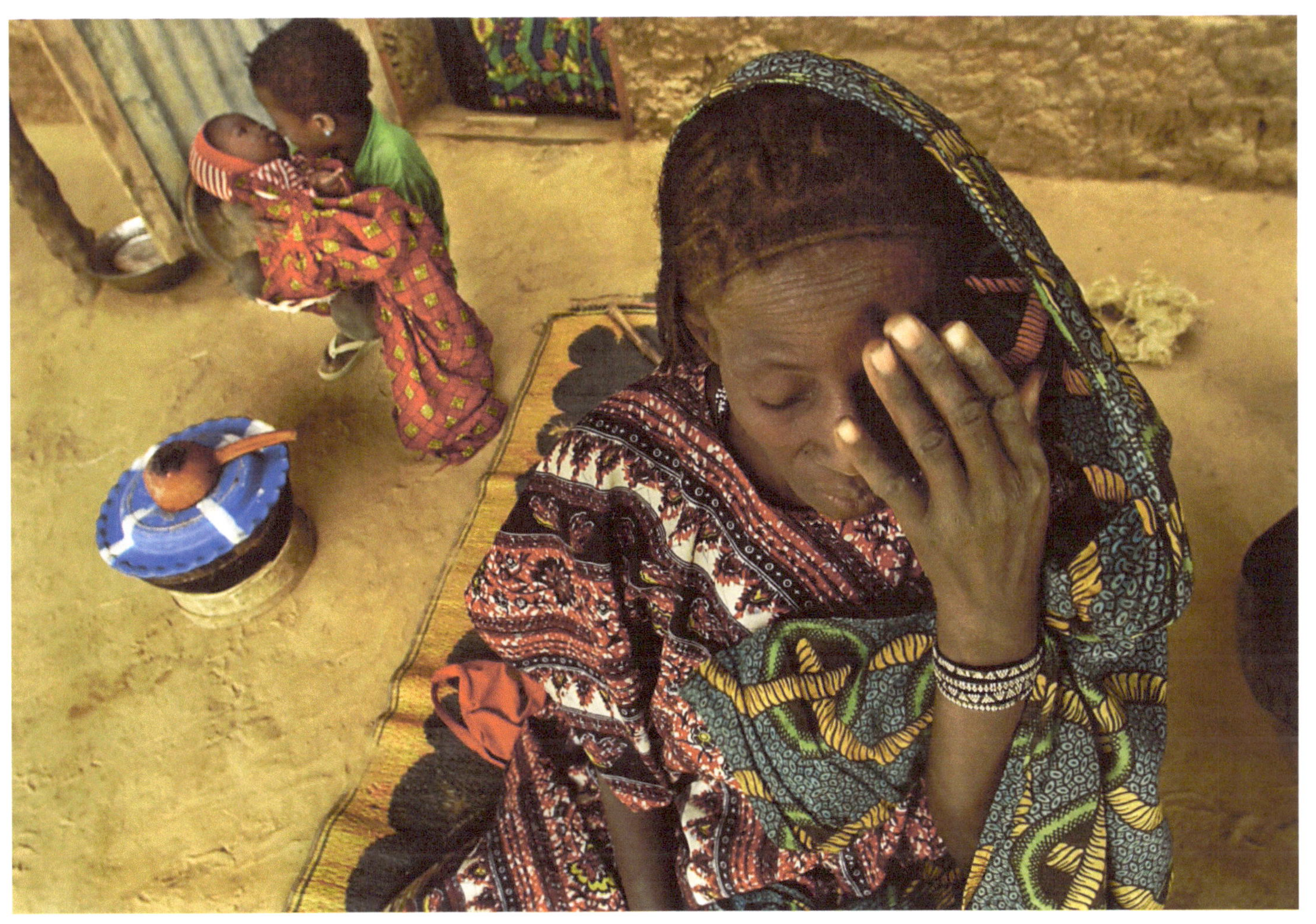

SCHWARZENEGGER CELEBRATES: Rabbi Boruch S. Cunin, left, Director of the west coast Chabad dances with California Governor Arnold Schwarzenegger, right, in an early Chanukah celebration at the State Capitol in Sacramento on Tuesday Dec. 20, 2005.

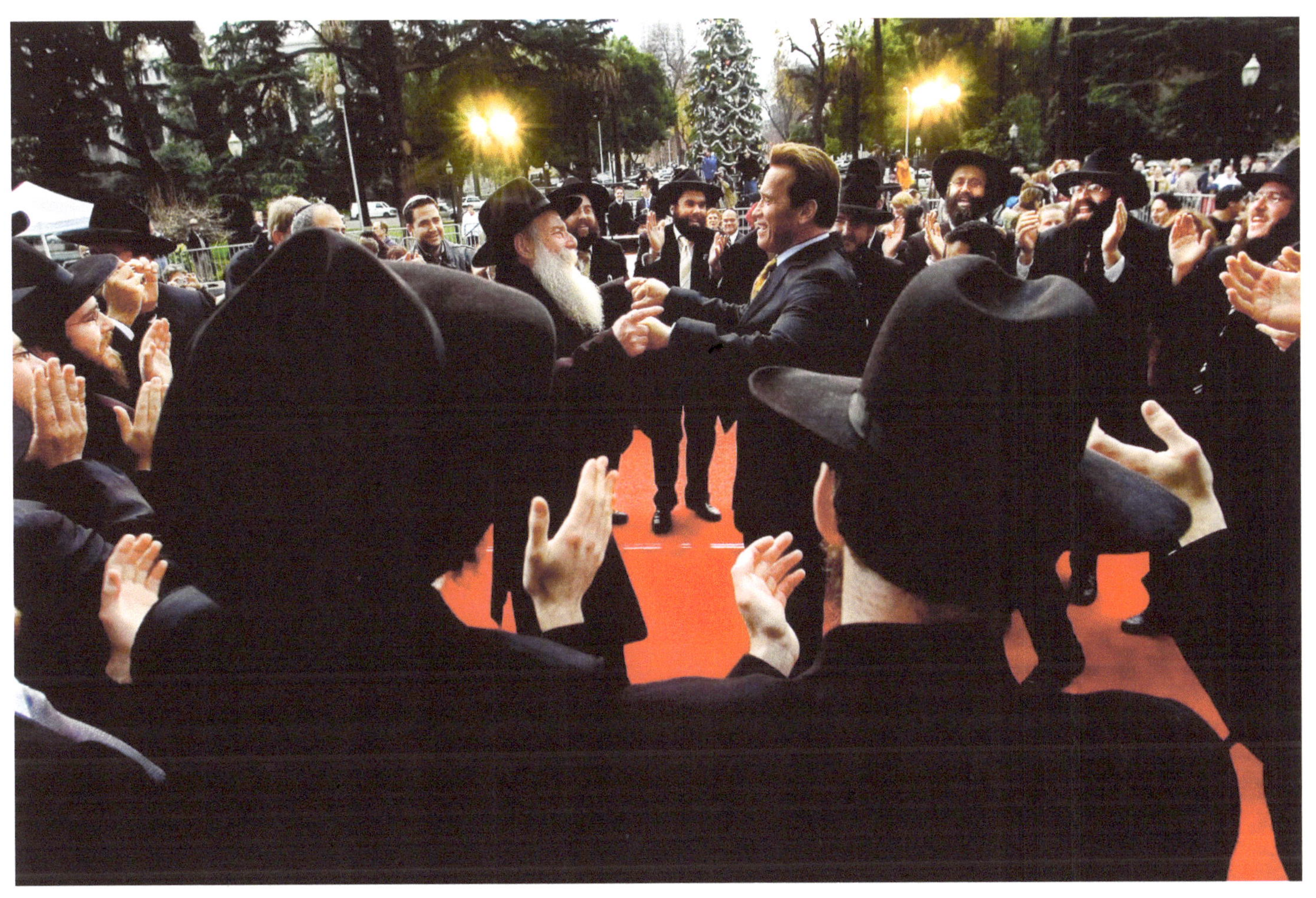

WOMEN AT WAR: California National Guard Spc. Melanie Zapata, 19, of Earlimart, CA, her wedding ring showing, holds her bullets during qualifications testing at Camp San Luis Obispo January 10, 2005. She says she won't hesitate to use her weapon in Iraq: "Do you want to come home alive or in a casket?" she says.

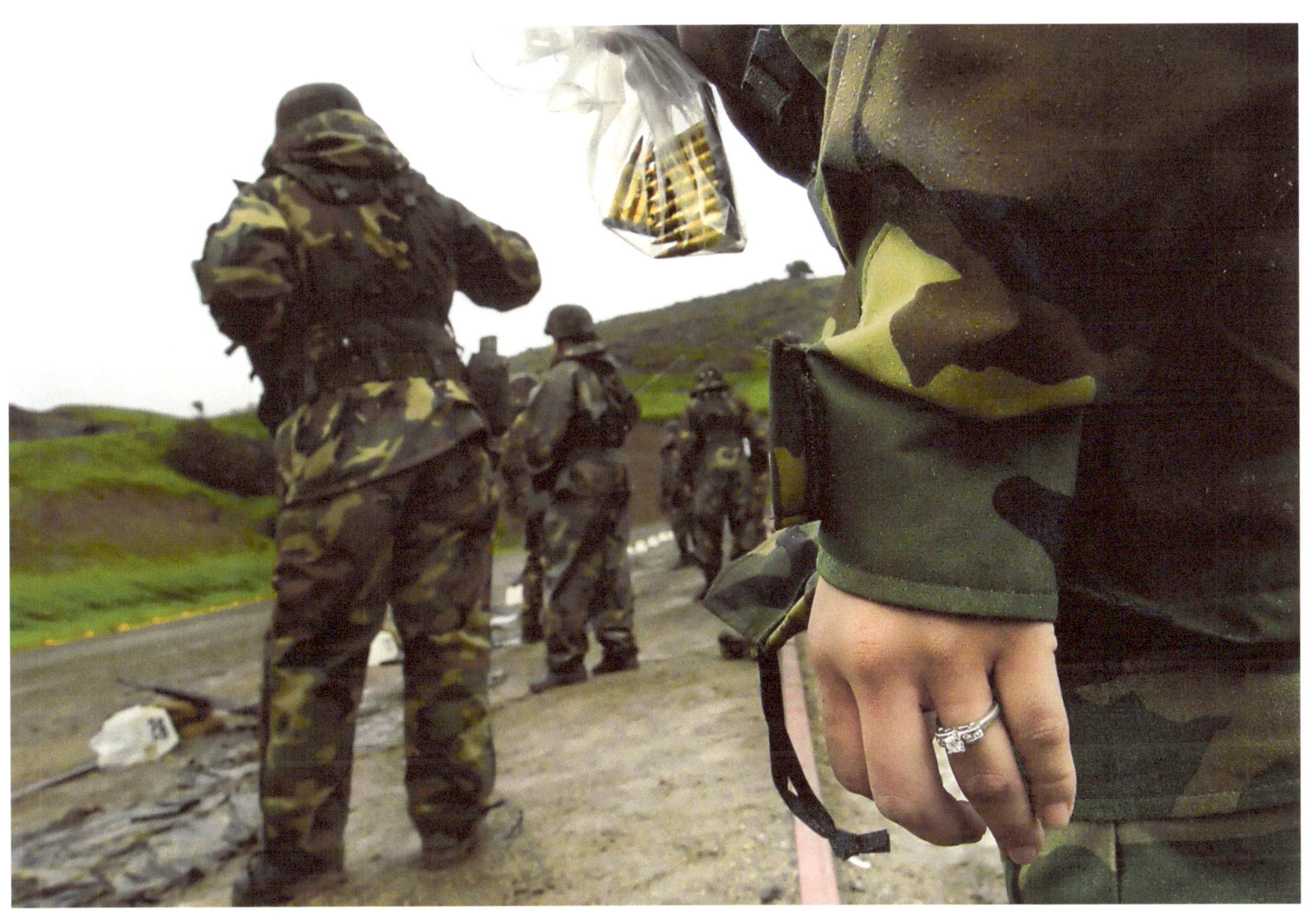

ACUTELY AUTISTIC BUT ALWAYS LOVED: Marlon Barton, 26, was diagnosed with autism when he was about 2, at a time when the condition was considered unusual and doctors offered little help or hope to parents of the children who suffered from it. His mother Pearlie Barton, 58, cares for him around the clock and worries about his future.

For reasons that are unclear, diagnoses have skyrocketed and the condition is surfacing in an estimated 1 in 150 children. As a tidal wave of these youngsters moves toward adulthood with complex behavioral and medical problems, society is largely unprepared. June 9, 2009.

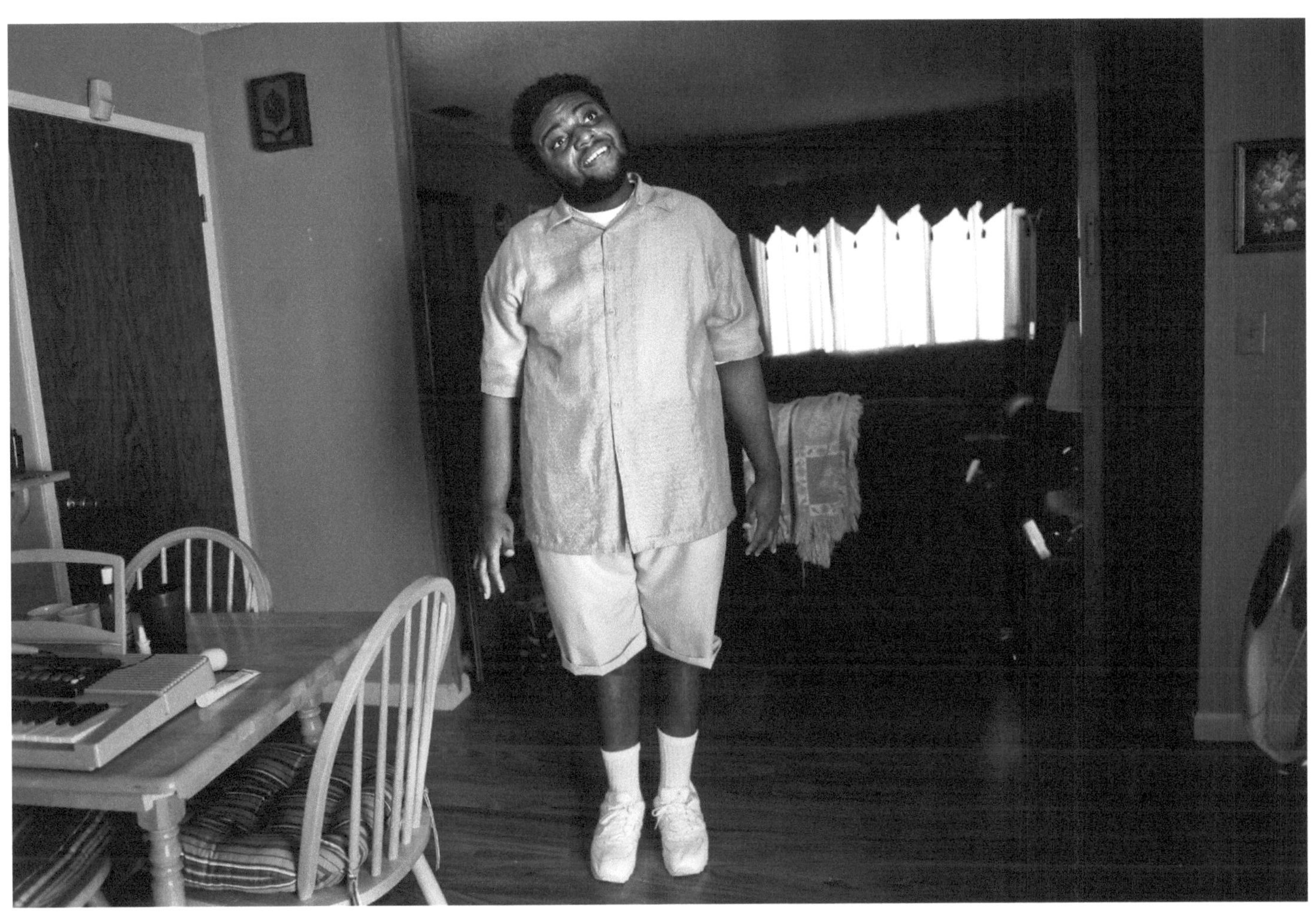

ACKNOWLEDGMENTS

Renée C. Byer's year-long documentary project was published as a four-part series in the Sacramento Bee and on the Internet as a multimedia package. "A Mother's Journey" won 17 international and national awards including the Pulitzer Prize in Feature Photography, a World Understanding Award, the Society of Professional Journalist's Sigma Delta Chi Award for Feature Photography, and the Casey Award for Meritorious Journalism, among many others. Its publication has led Ms. Byer on a whirlwind series of speaking engagements across America and the world.

The Samuel Dorsky Museum of Art (Dorsky Museum) has been delighted to be able to present Ms. Byers' photographs at the museum in conjunction with her April 2010 visiting professorship in the Journalism Program of the Department of Communication and Media at the State University of New York at New Paltz.

We welcomed this opportunity for the museum and Journalism Program to partner on the exhibition and related programs—and in the publication of this catalog.

On behalf of the Dorsky Museum of Art and the SUNY New Paltz Journalism Program, we wish to thank the following individuals whose determination that a publication should be created to memorialize the exhibition and draw attention to the story of Cyndie French and her son Derek Madsen led to the creation of this publication:

Arthur Anderson
James H. Ottaway, Jr. and Mary Ottaway

In addition, for their efforts in realizing the exhibition and coordinating the catalog publication, we thank:

Wayne Lempka, Collections Manager and Registrar, Dorsky Museum
Brian Wallace, Curator, Dorsky Museum
Bob Wagner, Preparator, Dorsky Museum
Arthur Zaczkiewicz, Catalog Publication Coordinator

Special thanks to Mark Morris, Multimedia Editor of the Sacramento Bee for his perfectionism overseeing the printing of the images for the exhibition.

Last but not least, we thank SUNY New Paltz President Steven G. Poskanzer for his vision and leadership and James H. Ottaway, Jr. for establishing the James H. Ottaway Sr. Endowed Professorship of Journalism, enabling us to bring this and other programs to the SUNY New Paltz campus.

Sara J. Pasti, Director, Samuel Dorsky Museum of Art
Rob Miraldi, Professor, Journalism Program, SUNY New Paltz and Ottaway Journalism Fellowship Coordinator

www.ingramcontent.com/pod-product-compliance
Lightning Source LLC
LaVergne TN
LVHW070829060826
844660LV00019B/990
9780615358451